Jack Charlton's World Cup Diary

JACK CHARLTON had a distinguished career as a centre back with Leeds United and England, with whom he won a World Cup medal at Wembley in 1966, before managing Sheffield Wednesday, Middlesbrough and Newcastle United. He became manager to the Republic of Ireland side in 1986 and has guided them to the most successful era in the history of Irish soccer.

PETER BYRNE has been a member of *The Irish Times* staff since 1960 and is Ireland's most travelled sports writer. He has covered six Olympic Games, three World Cups and a host of World Championships in all major sports. He has been Benson & Hedges Irish Sports Writer of the Year four times. He is married with three children and lives in Howth.

BILLY STICKLAND has covered all the major sports events of the 1980s and is Ireland's most distinguished sports photographer. Italia '90 was his second World Cup. Having worked purely as a freelance for some years, he founded Inpho which is Ireland's biggest and most successful sports picture agency.

Jack Charlton's World Cup Diary

with Peter Byrne

Photographs by Billy Stickland

GILL AND MACMILLAN

Published in Ireland by
Gill and Macmillan Ltd
Goldenbridge
Dublin 8
with associated companies in
Auckland, Delhi, Gaborone, Hamburg, Harare,
Hong Kong, Johannesburg, Kuala Lumpur, Lagos, London,
Manzini, Melbourne, Mexico City, Nairobi,
New York, Singapore, Tokyo
Text © Jack Charlton 1990
Photographs © Billy Stickland/Inpho 1990
Hardback 0 7171 1858 4
Paperback 0 7171 1788 X
Print origination by
Seton Music Graphics Ltd, Bantry, Co. Cork
Colour origination by
Kulor Centre Ltd, Dublin
Printed by
The Bath Press, Bath

Introduction

When we came home from Italy on 1 July, we got a reception in Dublin that none of us will ever forget. It could hardly have been better if we'd won the World Cup. It was also the end of a long, hard road.

That road had begun almost two years earlier when we played the first group qualifying match for Italia '90. By the autumn of 1989, only Northern Ireland and Malta stood between us and a place in Italy. This was when public expectation really began to rise and when I began to keep this diary.

This is how I recall those eight months from the Northern Ireland match in Lansdowne Road to the night in Rome's Olympic Stadium when we finally bowed out of the tournament, having established the Republic of Ireland as one of the eight best teams in the world. Also, thanks to our magnificent fans, Ireland had won a lot of new friends and admirers everywhere.

I have not gone back over my earlier impressions and opinions in the light of later events. Instead, I've let things stand as they seemed to me when they were first written.

So this is how I saw it unfold and develop. I hope that you enjoy remembering it with me.

Jack Charlton
August 1990

●

Ever since arriving in Dublin to take charge of the team for the return game against Northern Ireland at Lansdowne Road, I have sensed that things are different this time.

Like every other football enthusiast in Ireland, I have worked out the different permutations which would guarantee us a place in the World Cup finals in Italy. And the bottom line is that we need three points from our remaining two qualifying games with Northern Ireland and Malta to make mathematically certain that we will be among the 24 teams in the draw for the finals. So we all realised that we will be playing for big stakes against Billy Bingham's team. Still it doesn't explain away the tension which is making this a totally new experience for me.

The last thing I want is to go to Malta looking for a win in our concluding game to qualify. We desperately need to beat Northern Ireland to eliminate that hazard but I still can't come to terms with the tension among the players. Going into the home games against Spain and Hungary we knew we had to win both to stay on course for Italy. In each instance, we handled the pressure perfectly but now, for the first time, they are acting as if the occasion is getting to them. Frankly, it worries me.

In saying that, I am aware of the hype which affected even people with only a peripheral interest in football in Ireland this summer and autumn. Long before I became involved with the FAI in February 1986, there was a proud tradition of international football in this country. But I don't think anybody realised just how deep that passion ran until we qualified for the European championship finals in West Germany in 1988. That was an eye-opener for everybody, me included, and in a very real way, it has probably contributed to the pre-match nerves now.

From schoolboys to grandparents, showbusiness folk to people in religious orders, everybody seemed to be touched by the achievements of the Irish players in West Germany. And that, of course, worked wonders for national pride. It also served to lift the level of expectations. After years of frustration, the break-through had, at last, been achieved in the European championships. Now the fans demand that we qualify for the World Cup finals and the pressures are rising to a dangerous degree.

The task of any manager in this situation is to defuse the tension and settle his team. The point is that this is a game which I have always thought we will win. And any student of form in his full senses will, I think, agree with me. There are a lot of variables in football and I know from long years of bitter experience that you don't always win games which the critics regard as mere formalities. But looking at our team and the players available to Northern Ireland, I reckon there can only be one result to our game in Dublin—and I am hammering home the point at every team talk.

We played them in Belfast last year and while we were made to settle for a scoreless draw on the night, I saw nothing in that game which suggested that they would give us problems in Dublin. Most of the players who had served them so well in Spain in 1982 and again in Mexico four years later have now departed and with their going the team has ceased to be a major force in international football.

They have still retained Billy Bingham as manager, of course, and unquestionably he is Northern Ireland's biggest asset. I have a lot of respect for Billy as a manager. He reads the game well, knows how to motivate players and, given his modest resources, he worked wonders in getting his team to two World Cup finals.

But all managers, even the shrewdest, must have a base on which to work. And Billy, I think, went through an entire World Cup campaign without ever knowing where his real strength lay. In that situation, I reckoned that he needed a minor miracle to beat us at Lansdowne.

SATURDAY 7
October 1989

●

Because of the fact that England do not have a competitive game next Wednesday, there was a full Football League programme in England today. There were a few anxious hours before we knew that Ronnie Whelan and Andy Townsend would be available to join us.

Missing, of course, is Liam Brady and therein lies a story which has given the football writers in Ireland and England a lot of mileage in recent weeks.

Liam was substituted in the friendly game against West Germany in Dublin last month and was, apparently, so upset by my decision to take him off after only 36 minutes that he announced his decision to retire from international football later that evening.

The news created shock waves across the country. And with my hand on my heart, I can say that I understand perfectly the reasons why it has generated so much controversy.

Liam Brady had, truly, been one of the best players ever to come out of Ireland. I recall him in his early days at Arsenal as something of an artist, a hugely talented youngster who could almost make the ball talk with his left foot. Later he went to Italy and for seven seasons, he succeeded in imposing himself on one of the most competitive national championships in the world. That was longer than any other foreign player lasted in Italy in the eighties and, in a sense, it said much about the make-up of the man. Not only was he a superb player on the ball but his level of commitment to the game was total. And in a very real way, that made the parting all the more painful.

I am happy to say that our rift hasn't lasted. Within weeks we were corresponding with each other. That is the essence of sport and before long, I hope to be able to help him out with the arrangements for his testimonial.

Liam's tragedy was that at a time when he was at the summit of his career, the Republic of Ireland weren't qualifying for either the World Cup or European championship finals. And believe me, nobody deserved that stage more. Unfortunately, when the good times came for Ireland, circumstances contrived to rob him of that opportunity. I watched him only occasionally in the early stages of his international career but I doubt if he has ever played a better game for his country than in our final qualifying match for the 1988 European championship, against Bulgaria in Dublin in October 1987.

Brady was simply brilliant that day, covering, tackling, creating. And then, with the game won, he got himself sent off in the closing minutes. That was bad enough but in February of the following year even worse was to follow. Playing for West Ham in a game at Derby, he sustained a bad knee injury and effectively his season was over. It was cruel that at a time when Ireland most needed him, this gifted player was forced to watch the action in the European finals from the sideline.

I realised just how badly Liam wanted to play in those finals. But deep down, I suspected that it was only the start of his troubles. As a player, I once had a similar injury and I could identify precisely with the problems he was now experiencing.

I was younger than Brady at the time when I picked up the injury. But it still took me the greater part of a year to get over it. At 32, Liam, I felt, would have it all to do to get back to where he was in that remarkable game against Bulgaria. Yet the man's record and his special place in Irish football demanded that he be given the chance to prove that he could

still contribute to our World Cup challenge. The friendly with West Germany seemed the ideal occasion to put those claims to the test.

The Saturday before the game, I asked Maurice Setters to go and watch Liam play for West Ham. The word he brought back was not encouraging. In Maurice's opinion, Brady was gone as an international player but I still felt obliged to give Liam the chance of proving him wrong.

In fact, there were two other players who shared Liam Brady's challenge that day of proving that they could still do it for Ireland, Tony Galvin and Frank Stapleton. Galvin had done well, wonderfully well, for us in West Germany but after leaving Sheffield Wednesday for Swindon, the feeling was that his career was now in decline.

Frank, another of the enduring heroes of the game in this country, came back into English football last year after spells in Europe with Ajax of Amsterdam and Le Havre. In spite of his superb performances in the European finals, I still needed to be assured that he could do it for us.

All three players had a point to prove and I considered for a while the possibility of trying them in separate games. But after chewing on it for days, I eventually decided that the three of them would play against the West Germans. Had I been looking for a result in that game, I might have acted differently. But this was a friendly and the need to find out if the trio in question had a place in our plans for Italy superseded all other considerations.

Tony came through the test well. Frank, in many respects, was even better but, sadly, Liam didn't do it for us and I took him off before half-time. If I am absolutely honest, I've got to say that I was a little cold-blooded in what I did. That said, I would have put the other players and, ultimately, the game itself at risk if I had left him in the side.

Brady's natural style of play was often at odds with the type of game we favour. His natural instincts are to bring the ball from defence and play it out, whereas our tactics demanded that he take it from the front and go from there. This was particularly noticeable in the West German game in which I had to anchor Paul McGrath in midfield to compensate for the gaps Brady was leaving. That unbalanced us across the middle and when the Germans cancelled out Stapleton's early goal, I decided to act and bring in Andy Townsend. Some people argued that I should not have made the change until half-time. Had I taken this course of action, however, we might well have conceded a second goal before the break and at that point, the way back could have been impossible.

As it transpired, Townsend's arrival altered the pattern of the match. The opposition caused us considerably fewer problems in the second half and with a little luck, we might even have won it.

WEDNESDAY 11
October 1989

●

Apart from everything else, that substitution proved what a useful player Andy is. So it is a worry to discover that together with McGrath and Moran, he has been in the wars before today's game.

I can cater for change in other areas of the team but central midfield is crucial. When you alter this part, you change the whole structure and, as a consequence, the performance of the team. I know our capabilities and what I can expect from the players when my middle line is settled. But if I have to tamper with the structure, I am always conscious that I am heading into unknown territory.

McGrath, as I suspected, didn't make it in time for the game but, fortunately, Moran and Townsend did. And once they had been cleared to play, the team virtually picked itself. This was a job for experienced professionals. I knew that I had a tried and trusted team, one that had served me well in the preceding months and I wasn't about to change it.

In fact, they didn't play particularly well in the first half. Billy Bingham had done his homework well and in the early stages, they didn't settle on the ball, thereby denying us the chance of closing them down. Instead of playing the ball out, Northern Ireland took us on at our own game by knocking it back over our heads. And it frustrated us so much that we began to lose our rhythm.

Normally, we play what I call the in-and-out game. By playing the ball into the corners, you put the opposition under pressure but now, inexplicably, our players were reversing that tactic by knocking the ball in from wide angles in the hope of hitting Tony Cascarino with the cross. It didn't work, mainly because the big QPR lad, Alan McDonald, was having a blinder. McDonald, not so clever when the ball is behind him, is still a good player coming forward and Tony was getting nothing from him.

I was worried then and more so when Northern Ireland almost scored in two hair-raising moments in the space of little more than a minute. Twice our defence was pulled apart and Michael O'Neill had chances of putting the ball in Paddy Bonner's net. A goal at that point might have been disastrous for us. Had Northern Ireland gone in front, they would have settled into what I consider their normal pattern of competing in their own penalty area and inviting us to come at them. By dropping one of their centre forwards back into a defensive position, they could have made it difficult for us to claw our way back into the game.

The first score was always going to be vital and, luckily, it came our way just before half-time. Cascarino competed with the goalkeeper and the centre backs for a long ball from Steve Staunton and when it fell kindly for Ronnie Whelan, he put it away without any fuss. On reflection, it was basically the product of the goalkeeper's mistake in coming too far off his line. But these are the kind of errors you hope and pray for—and it put us firmly in the driving seat.

Half-time in our dressing room was something special today. Generally, I try to be as constructive as possible in my talks at the break. I speak to the players collectively for two or three minutes and then talk with them individually pointing out the little things that are going wrong and more frequently encouraging them in what they are doing right.

But this was different. I was angry with what I had just seen and I had a bigger go at them than in any game since I took charge. We had been lulled into playing the game that Billy wanted us to play and we were suffering for it. The bottom line in my talk was unmistakable. We had got where we were by playing a certain type of game. Why, oh why, change the pattern on this of all days? I told them that we needed to get the ball in behind the centre backs and turn them. And in the second half, we did.

Within two minutes of the restart, I knew that the message had got through. Whelan played a long ball inside the full back to Tony. He laid it off for Kevin Sheedy and suddenly the space which had been denied us in the first half opened up. For the next 25 minutes or so, I thought we played some good football and were not flattered by further goals from Ray Houghton and Cascarino. Then we relaxed and I found myself shouting at them once more. Mick McCarthy, I recall, got a little upset with me but I was unrepentant. Football, for me, is a 90-minute game and you give it your best shot until the last kick of the match.

Now, as I saw it, our players were closing up shop with 20 minutes to go and settling for a win of three goals. That didn't please me one little bit. I was only too well aware that there was another game scheduled to be played in our group in the World Cup today and despite what people were saying I was not going to take anything for granted.

Sure, Hungary had a vastly inferior goals difference to us and it would have required a minor miracle on their part to rush four or five goals past Spain, even on their own ground and in front of their own supporters in Budapest. But I had lived long enough to realise that in football, nothing is for certain. In this sport, you cannot depend on anybody doing you favours and my gut feeling at Lansdowne Road was to grind Northern Ireland into the ground and score as many as possible. I honestly thought we could have put away another two or three goals had we concentrated and played out the full 90 minutes. But then, who can quibble with a 3–0 win?

The mood of the crowd at the end of the game was ecstatic. For them, this was the real World Cup qualifier and now that we had won it, they regarded our place in the finals as certain. I was probably in a minority of one, leaving the ground that day, who reckoned that there was still work to be done. I hoped and believed that we would go to Italy but at the back of my mind was this terrible thought that Spain, with their place in the World Cup finals already secured, might be less than fully competitive in their game against the Hungarians. Back in the team's hotel, a big crowd of supporters had already assembled by the time we

arrived there and I noticed among other things a television crew. They had obviously come to do a story on the Irish team qualifying for the finals but far from reassuring me, that only heightened the feeling that something could yet go wrong.

On this occasion, I had broken with custom and taken my wife Pat to stay with me at the team hotel. Normally, when she came to Ireland, she stayed with Des Casey's wife at their home in Dundalk and that suited me.

I don't go along with the idea of players' wives staying at our hotel and if I laid down one rule for them, it would obviously be grossly unfair to make another to suit myself. This time, however, I decided that I wanted Pat to be with me.

We went directly to our room on our return, the intention being to stay away from the media people until I knew the result of the Budapest game which started some four hours after ours. It was to be a long and nail-biting evening, spent in front of a television set, waiting on the magical word from Hungary. The game wasn't televised live but the RTE people in the hotel were, apparently, in contact by phone with Budapest. And when Mick Byrne, our trainer, came into our room to tell us that Spain were leading 1–0 at half-time, I began to feel a little less tense.

The Spaniards were, plainly, intent on doing the business and while I had no idea how the game was going, apart from knowing the scoreline, I figured that there was no way back for Hungary. And if they lost, we were through.

Shortly afterwards, we learned that Spain had scored a second time and I thought to myself, great—now we can have a real celebration party. Then somebody told us that Hungary had pulled one back and it was sweating time again. The next 20 minutes or so felt like an hour and I remember saying to Pat how strange it was that the bush telegraph had gone silent. Surely, Hungary hadn't equalised or, worse still, won. Then, there was this almighty thump on the door and when I opened it, Mick Byrne was standing there, grinning, with the television people directly behind him. My first impression was that Spain had held on for the win and I couldn't believe it when they told me that the Hungarians had hit back to draw 2–2.

It wasn't the result I wanted and I could see no reason at all for the elation around me. At that moment, I didn't want to face the cameras and the television people left. Later, when I went down to the foyer of the hotel, I discovered that the fans were in party mood and that equaliser or no equaliser, they were ready to pop the champagne corks.

But at the risk of being called a spoil-sport, I am not yet ready to join in the celebrations—and I've told them so. The job we had started in Belfast 13 months ago isn't over. Malta might yet tell a story.

11–14 NOVEMBER
1989

●

Ever since the dates were announced for our World Cup qualifying programme, I have been looking forward with relish to the prospect of taking the team to Malta. Not that playing football on the island is any big deal. The Maltese have never been among the better teams in the game and fellow pros speak with horror of the state of the ground in Valetta in the bad old days. But this is the occasion I plan to celebrate our coming of age by making certain of our place in the finals. And nothing, bar nothing, is going to stop us. There has, however, been a last-minute snag.

The snag was that with the big day nearly dawning, I almost wasn't there. Last week's newspapers, consumed by the mathematical permutations which would take us into the draw for Italy, didn't carry the story. The truth is, however, that in the week before we were to set off for Valetta, I found myself in a situation in which I came close to having to resign as manager of the Republic of Ireland team.

Fortunately, it didn't come to that but had it done so, it would have been among my saddest days in football. I have never made any secret of the job satisfaction I receive with Ireland and the thought that I might have to give it up because of circumstances outside my control appalled me.

When I applied for the post in the first instance, I did so because it offered me the chance of a fresh challenge at a time when I had become totally disillusioned with club management. To some, a club job may look attractive but, you can take my word for it, there is a lot of drudgery attaching to it as well.

I have never been an office manager in the football sense. The idea of sitting back in a chair and allowing others to do the routine things like coaching and checking out players was not for me. I had to be involved but I wasn't long in the business before I stumbled on the bitter truth that it was a seven-days-a-week job. For much of the time, it was a case of travelling up and down England, watching three or four games a week, looking at my players and keeping an eye on others who might one day sign for me. In that kind of environment, it is easy to lose sight of the fact that there is another world outside football.

Besides, the structure of the game was fast changing and I didn't like much of what I saw. When a manager went to sign a player in the old days, it was a relatively straightforward routine of a chat, a cup of tea, perhaps, and the deal was done. But things had moved on to such a degree in the '80s that if you wished to do business, you had to have an accountant, a solicitor and sometimes a doctor in on the discussions. This was not the game I knew and I resented it.

The Ireland appointment was vastly different. I was no longer working with players on a daily basis but rather borrowing them from club managers six or seven times a year. Over three seasons, I had built up a good rapport with those players and as the element of togetherness grew, I valued the relationship that much more.

It is always a joy for a manager to work with good material and while the responsibilities are that much greater, the rewards of international football in terms of fulfilment can be enormous. It was against that background that the tension began to build in the run-up to the Malta game.

It had all to do with sponsorship and the players' rights to market themselves. This forms an important part of footballers' incomes at times of World Cup and European championship finals when the commercial sector is keen to cash in on the publicity hype. The problem now, as the players saw it, was that the right was in danger of being taken from them.

Opel had been the official sponsors of the Irish team ever since I became involved and by virtue of their support at a time when it wasn't particularly fashionable to back the game, had rendered Irish football a tremendous service. Under the terms of their contract with the FAI, they reserved the right to use their logo on the shirts in team photographs.

Other firms now wanted a slice of that action and one in particular, the Irish Permanent Building Society, was anxious to undertake an advertising campaign built around a picture of the squad. When Opel sought a High Court injunction restraining them from doing so, the players saw it as a move which would restrict their earning power and reacted accordingly.

My views in these matters had always been clear. From lunch-time on Monday, right through to the end of the game on Wednesday, the players were under my control and, by extension, that of the FAI. What they did in their own time was their business and if they could make extra money from promotions and product endorsement, good luck to them. The Opel–Irish Permanent dispute was, however, particularly complicated and it happened at the wrong time as far as I was concerned.

I was under pressure to give the go-ahead for various commercial projects, billing us as World Cup finalists even before we qualified. I always believed we would win the game in Malta but at the same time, I was reluctant to tempt fate by presuming that our place in the finals was assured. It was a tricky decision but conscious of the needs of the advertisers to get their act together and launch their promotions without further delay, I eventually agreed. Now the problem was aggravated by the fact that Opel sponsored a function at which the 'Player of the Year' awards were made in Dublin last Sunday, the night before we went to Malta. Naturally, they wanted the members of the squad to be present.

As team manager, it was my responsibility to ensure that they actually turned up. But in the middle of last week, I was told that they weren't going to show up at the function. In those circumstances, I believed that I was being forced into a situation in which I would have no option but to resign.

I have always tried to be fair to everybody, the players, the FAI and the general public. But I've always insisted on exercising control. If you are the boss, you must act like the boss.

As such, I was determined that, dispute or no dispute, I would insist on the players' attendance at the awards dinner. The message I was getting from those supposed to be in the know was that they weren't coming and the more I thought

of it, the more certain I became that I would find myself in a position with no room for manoeuvre. In that case, I would have to quit.

As it transpired, it never did come down to that. On Friday, I phoned Frank Stapleton in Manchester and was never more relieved to hear anybody say yes. Frank told me that the players were ready to honour any commitment they had made and they would, of course, do as I asked. Afterwards, I learned that there had never been any doubt about their intentions, proving yet again that it isn't always wise to listen to tip-offs. But that, unquestionably, was my most uncomfortable experience as Irish manager.

Kevin Moran was adjudged as the outstanding senior player of the year, Steve Staunton got the Under-21 award and I had no argument with either choice. I went back to our hotel and slept the sleep of the contented.

FRIDAY 10 NOVEMBER
1989

●

This game is not really worrying me. We beat Malta 2–0 when we played them in Dublin last May and I saw nothing that day to suggest that even on home territory, they can trouble us now.

Additionally, they are now going to have to improvise in the absence, through suspension, of two of their best players, goalkeeper David Cluett and Raymond Vella. Vella looked a good player when I saw him at Lansdowne although his loss, I reckon, would make no real difference. Irrespective of the team Malta field, we should have their measure.

More worrying for me, by far, had been the fact that the Spain–Hungary game in Seville the same day was originally scheduled to kick off after our game. As matters stand in Group Six, Spain still need a point to make certain of topping the table. But from our viewpoint, it is more important that Hungary should lose. If the original match arrangements had survived, and depending on the result from Valetta, the Spanish manager, Luis Suarez could, as I might have done, put an experimental team on the pitch. For all Spain's depth in strength, that would have placed the game at risk for them. By insisting that the two games be played simultaneously, however, FIFA have indirectly applied pressure on Suarez to save at least a point. I can breathe a little more easily.

Mick McCarthy, troubled yet again by his knees, is not being considered for selection but in a nice gesture which typifies our special set-up, the FAI have decided to take him along as their guest. The fans might not realise it, but one of the most stressful parts of my job is sitting by the telephone on Saturday evenings waiting for the grim word from club managers that such and such a player had been injured earlier in the day and would not be available to join us. That threat, happily, has not materialised for the Maltese game and, for once, supply is surplus to demand.

Although all our established players with the exception of McCarthy have travelled

with us, we still have some niggling doubts about the fitness of Ronnie Whelan, John Aldridge, Tony Cascarino and Andy Townsend. Because of that, I won't give my team to newsmen until just before the match.

Normally, I inform journalists of the team I intend to play the day before the game. By that stage, of course, I will have told the players themselves of my plans and they never, ever, learn the team from the press. Because of the doubts surrounding Whelan and Townsend, in particular, it is now necessary to abandon that practice and keep everybody guessing until kick-off time.

Apart from everything else, I have a couple of delicate team choices to make and they involve Paul McGrath. Paul had always been one of the key men in my team and from day one, I saw him as a player who would give me some valuable options. I have always believed in the concept of playing people who can double as centre backs in the centre of midfield. The logic is simple. When cover is required at full back, the centre back will automatically go across to provide it. You then need somebody to drop back and fill the space in the centre and this responsibility, I find, is best undertaken by those with experience in the position. Mark Lawrenson was another player capable of doing this job for us but, sadly, injury cut short his career at a time when he had still so much to give. Mark is a hell of a loss—imagine how he would have performed in the World Cup finals—but we are extremely fortunate in being able to call on a player of the quality of McGrath to fill the position.

Paul missed the Northern Ireland game, of course, and afterwards experienced a few personal problems. In that situation, I am intent on playing him in Malta but the problem is—in which position?

I am also anxious to include Andy Townsend. For a while, I considered the possibility of leaving Paul in the centre and switching Townsend to the left side of midfield in place of Kevin Sheedy.

Eventually, I have decided to play McGrath at right back and leave out Chris Morris. Before I did, I had a word with Chris and explained what I was about. Nobody likes being told that he is out of the side but if a manager takes the time to sit down with the player and give him the reasons for his decision, he will get no argument in 90 per cent of cases.

15 NOVEMBER
1989

●

The most striking thing about today's game was the frustration of dominating the Maltese and yet scoring only twice. In the opening quarter alone, we could have hit three but a combination of bad luck and good goalkeeping kept us out.

Just as Billy Bingham did in Dublin a month ago, Malta tried to take a leaf out of our book by lofting the ball back over our heads, and gave us a few surprising problems in the opening 15 minutes. The difference is that while British players are capable of keeping that kind of game going, the Europeans invariably lapse back into their old pattern of playing it out short from defence. I suspected that sooner or later Malta would make the same mistake and sure enough, they did.

Gradually, they began to dwell on the ball at the back and when they did, we pounced. In a matter of minutes the tide turned and as we began to force them into more and more errors, even the home supporters must have suspected that their team was about to come undone.

When the goal eventually arrived, it was the product of a set-piece move we had practised diligently. Kevin Sheedy took the corner kick on the left, Tony Cascarino headed it on at the near post and there was John Aldridge waiting to do the rest. It was Aldo's first goal in a competitive international and I could not have been happier for him. For three years or more, he had waited to savour that moment and, along the way, taken some stick from sections of the press for his failure to reproduce his Liverpool form for Ireland. That was nonsense. I never felt under any pressure to drop him and the fans agreed with me. Those that didn't were guilty of misunderstanding our style and the particular type of game we play.

In our match plan, we employ a target man up front and a runner to get to the knock-ons. Tony Cascarino, Frank Stapleton and Niall Quinn are all capable of doing the first job but our options for the second role are considerably fewer.

Young David Kelly, at one time, looked capable of doing it but after scoring three times on his first international appearance against Israel at Dalymount, he hadn't developed as I thought he would on leaving Walsall for West Ham.

It is not an easy assignment by any stretch of the imagination and that is why I admire Aldo so much. When the ball is knocked in behind the opposing defence, it is his responsibility to get to it first or, alternatively, close down if a defender has it. By definition, he is required to work across the width of the park for us, a huge change from the role he filled at Liverpool where, more often than not, he was to be found in and around the six yards area. As a consequence, his chances of hitting the target for Ireland were much more limited than those at Anfield. And given the higher quality of international football in situations in which, ringed by five or six defenders, a striker must make his first touch count, I never really expected him to flood us with goals. But now that he has broken his duck in a World Cup game—he scored in the friendly game against Tunisia before that—I hope that it will boost his confidence.

Thanks to John's goal, we were well on the way to victory at half-time but I still wasn't pleased. Considering all the possession we had enjoyed, a 1–0 lead was scarcely flattering and we certainly needed another score to make it safe. Chris Morris got into the game after all as a replacement when Kevin Moran walked over to the bench and told me that he couldn't go on because of a groin injury. There is no braver player in the game than Kevin and when he tells you that he is injured, you know, for sure, that he is not exaggerating. With Moran gone, I

switched Paul McGrath to centre back and brought in Chris Morris as right back. Paul, as ever, did a good job for us there and Chris, given the opportunity to overlap, showed yet again what a fine attacking player he can be. No less than young Steve Staunton in the other full back position, Chris has known the sharp end of my tongue on occasions. Above all else, I want my full backs to get tight on to their wingers for there is no point in John Aldridge chasing his heart out to close down people at the other end of the field if his teammates are going to undo it by standing off.

Morris and Staunton tend to do that too often and it gets them into trouble. Chris, at times, seems more interested in filling the hole than in tight marking and I can see no valid reason for that. If by any chance the winger knocks the ball past him, he is fast enough in recovery to get back.

But in Malta, at least, it has not really mattered. We always had the game firmly under control in the second half and in due course the goal which clinched our 2–0 win materialised. Andy Townsend, moving quickly on to a throw-in, carved his way through the centre of the Maltese defence and when he was brought down in the penalty area, Aldo, with a double sway of the hips, made penalty taking look easy.

The general view is that it hasn't been a great game but it was the one which eventually cleared the road to Rome for us. Right from the moment we beat Spain in Dublin, I had always reckoned that we would qualify. But it was still a great

Making a point at the training session before the Northern Ireland match.

Sometimes you've just got to let fly!

Tony Cascarino, Andy Townsend and Ray Houghton in action against Northern Ireland.

△   David O'Leary and John Aldridge in happy mood before the Malta game.

△   The world's best supporters in Valetta.

Aldo after his first goal in Valetta.

We're there! Ronnie Whelan and myself after the win against Malta.

experience to walk into our dressing room after the match in Valetta today and savour with the players our hour of success.

By qualifying for the finals, they have secured for themselves a worldwide stage and that is no more than they deserve. Resuming where they had left off in the Euro finals, they have proved their character in eight qualifying games of contrasting quality and excitement. Now they are about to reap the rewards.

For me, as somebody remarked, it is a chance to revisit my youth. As a player, I was fortunate enough to share with Bobby in the thrill of winning a World Cup medal with England at Wembley in 1966.

Now I am going back to the finals as a manager. I wonder how the two experiences will measure up. When you are playing, you worry and fret about a big game right up to the time of the kick-off. Then the whistle goes and you become totally immersed in your own game. Football management is different. Whereas a player is responsible, primarily, for looking after himself, the boss must take on board the problems and the challenges of every member of his team. And that is as true of junior football as it is of World Cup competition.

I will never attempt to draw a comparison between the job satisfaction of player and manager. The two are totally different but sitting there with the team in the dressing room today, I felt a real glow of fulfilment.

No less than the players, I was also acutely aware of the need to involve our supporters in the celebrations. Throughout the campaign, they had been simply magnificent, travelling in strength to away games and giving us the vocal backing that made us almost unbeatable in Dublin.

This was their triumph as much as ours and I wanted them to know it. Long before the Malta game, Opel had thought of flying in a top Irish band for an open air concert in Valetta but after inspecting the city, they decided it wasn't feasible. The Barley Corn folk group did turn up at the game and for 30 minutes or so until darkness fell, they entertained the crowd from the sideline. I think the Maltese fans got a lot more enjoyment out of that performance than they did from the game.

Incidentally, I don't think our supporters have got the best deal in Malta—and remember, many of them have made big sacrifices, travelling through the fog which has shut down airports in Ireland and Britain, to get here. We had planned on staying at one particular hotel which had the space and the facilities to stage a hooley after the match. Unfortunately, however, we discovered that it had been pre-booked. The hotel in which we have eventually settled, lacks those facilities and, worse still, implements a tight security operation which has prevented many of the supporters getting in. I feel genuinely sorry about that.

Yet, we managed to salvage something from the night when we went out into the town and joined them there. The mood was merry and I was even inveigled into a few bars of Dublin In The Rare Oul' Times.

In football, as in much else, the occasions for real celebration, are not all that many.

But given the special significance of the day for Irish football, I believed that this was one of them. And we did.

SUNDAY 10
December 1989

●

Sophia Loren I had always regarded as a nice woman. I knew less about Luciano Pavarotti but he sounded and looked fine any time he appeared on my television set. That was until yesterday's draw for the World Cup finals in Rome when, suddenly I began to see two of Italy's favourite people in a slightly different perspective.

Not that either of them was directly responsible for the rotten draw we got. But for me, they will always be identified with an afternoon when the magic of the World Cup began to go a little sour for us. Yesterday, in common with thousands of Irish supporters, I discovered that lightning can indeed strike twice. We have ended up for the second time in two years in a group which includes England and Holland. The fact that Egypt are also in there with us seems almost irrelevant. Because of the hooliganism of a section of their support, England and Holland had been regarded as the booby prize by each of the other 22 countries in the draw. That we should finish up playing both of them is a fate almost too cruel to be true.

In a sense, it was the logical culmination of a difficult period for me. I had thought for some time about going to Rome for the draw—and then decided against it. The majority of the other team managers, including Bobby Robson, travelled there and to some people it seemed natural that I should join them. After looking into the pros and cons, however, I reckoned no. The prospect of being waylaid by a small army of journalists, sticking tape recorders into my face in their quest for reaction to the draw didn't exactly appeal to me. And besides, Opel, our sponsors, had arranged to hold a reception in Dublin to coincide with the television programme which was due to be beamed live from Italy. I was aware of the tremendous interest in Ireland in the countdown to the draw and, on balance, the prospect of spending time with friends in Dublin was a lot more attractive than being in Rome.

Even before the groups were drawn, a couple of important meetings of FIFA officials took place in the Italian capital and one of them had a direct bearing on our team. A meeting of the organising committee of Italia '90 was due to rule on the question of the eligibility of those players who had received two yellow cards in the preliminary stages of the championship to participate in the finals. Normally, a double booking means an automatic one-match ban but in previous World Cup finals a general amnesty had been declared and the slate wiped clean for those involved. From our point of view, it was essential that the tradition be maintained for we had Ray Houghton on two yellows after his name had gone into the referee's notebook in Malta.

At one point, our apprehension was still higher for a report appeared in the press that John Aldridge, previously carded in the game against Northern Ireland, had also been disciplined in Valetta. That, eventually, turned out to be a case of mistaken identity but with Houghton in jeopardy, the situation was still worrying. From the early days of my involvement with the Irish team, Ray had been an important part of our plans. Together with John Aldridge, he won his first cap against Wales in Dublin in March 1986 and while we lost that game to a goal scored by Ian Rush, I reckoned that we had stumbled on two nuggets.

I was even more convinced when I went to Wembley the following month and watched Houghton and Aldridge fill important roles in Oxford's 3–0 success over QPR in the League Cup final. Houghton, in particular, had a magnificent game that day and I left London more convinced than ever of his ability to make up into a top-class international player. Events were, of course, to prove me right. Ray is the kind of player that every manager likes to have in his team, a lad who is willing to cover every blade of grass on the field and yet sharp enough to get on to the final ball where it matters most, in the penalty area. More than most, perhaps, he is a man who thrives on the big occasion, be it for Liverpool or for Ireland, and the thought that we might have to replace him for our first game in Italy was made that much blacker by the fact that it could necessitate a major reshuffle of the team

The right side of midfield is not the easiest position for us to fill in an emergency but, ironically, an option presented itself at the start of the season when I brought Gary Waddock back into the squad for the first time in three years for the game against West Germany. Gary had made a number of appearances for Ireland when Eoin Hand was in charge but then suffered a bad injury which threatened to put him out of the game permanently. But the lad is nothing if not brave and when I saw him at the end of the 1988-89 season, I was astounded by the manner in which he had fought his way back to fitness. I like the look of Waddock. He is a busy type on the pitch, puts his foot in and, very importantly, gets between players in the opposing team. In that, he is not unlike Ray Houghton and had it been necessary, he might have provided useful cover for the Liverpool player.

As it happened, it was decided to implement the amnesty for the booked players and, frankly, I would have been shocked if it were otherwise. If FIFA insisted in carrying over yellow cards to the finals, it would have conferred an unfair advantage on Italy and Argentina who, as hosts and holders respectively, were not required to qualify.

With that matter settled, I arrived in Dublin in a relaxed mood to look forward to a draw which was going to colour all our thoughts for much of the next year. When you get to this stage of the championship, there is no such thing as an easy touch. In theory, at least, the names of the best teams in the world are going into those infamous glass jars and in that situation, you prepare yourself for the worst. Yet there were, inevitably, certain taboos. Even before a ball had been kicked in the finals, the suspicion was that the heat and humidity of an Italian summer would prove a crucial factor. The preference among the great majority of European managers was for a venue in the northern part of the country. Additionally, I did not want to meet up again so soon with any of the teams we had played in the European championship in West Germany—certainly not in the first phase of the finals. I was not to know it then, but before long I would be disillusioned on both counts.

I watched the draw in the company of 150 people in the Burlington Hotel with a mixture of impatience and bewilderment. Ever since we knew for certain that we were going to the finals, all of us had heard stories of how the draw would be arranged to suit certain teams. One West German television station, for example, was so convinced that we would be placed in the same group as them, that they dispatched a film crew to Dublin to get our reaction when it was officially confirmed. For them, no less than us, the next 90 minutes or so would hold a few surprises.

I don't know how the West Germans felt but I reckoned that the people who put together the television programme got their priorities all wrong. The big event taking place in Rome was all about football. Yet, for the better part of an hour, we had to look at dancers, singers and children waving flags while we waited for the real action to take place. It was, for all the world, a concert.

By the time they got down to the actual business of drawing the teams, I was just about as uncomfortable, sitting in that room, as the manager of a team losing 6–0. Lined up in front of me was a battery of cameras, all ready to take the shot which would fit some smart caption in the papers.

If I'd put my hand to my head, they would have said I was worrying. Had I yawned, it would have been interpreted as boredom. So, I just sat there as motionless as possible. And it hurt. Inevitably, by the time the papers hit the streets next morning, some of the photographers had caught me momentarily off guard. But bad as the draw turned out for us, those pictures had less to do with football than coincidence.

Was the draw pre-arranged or did FIFA leave it all to pure chance? You can make up your own mind on that but if it was fixed, all I can say is that I was watching a bloody magician in action. There were, I know, gasps all round when Italy emerged in probably the easiest of the six groups. And just as everybody had predicted, Spain finished up in the same section as Belgium. Was that down to luck or was it something else?

The eyes of the world were trained on those six jars. And as such, it is difficult to see how anybody, no matter how skilful, could have manipulated the names on those slips of paper which were held directly in front of the cameras. One point struck me, however, as odd. The six football celebrities, including Pele and my old England teammate, Bobby Moore, who reached into the jars and took out the balls containing the slips, did not, actually, open them. That job was performed by Sepp Blatter, FIFA's general secretary, who then proceeded to call out the names of the countries involved.

Another point which baffled me was the seedings. I could understand perfectly why the top six seeds should have been kept apart. But that ought to have been that. Instead, we were told shortly before they started pulling from the jars, that two South American countries, Uruguay and Colombia would be separated for 'geographical' reasons. If that was the sole consideration, what about the different European countries playing each other? More to the point, why put the Republic of Ireland and England in the same group? To make matters worse, the Uruguayans and the Colombians were both involved with us in the third flight of seedings. It didn't need a professor of mathematics to tell me that it reduced our options considerably. As it turned out, the third seeds were the last to be drawn and as the alternatives began to dwindle, the grim realisation dawned that FIFA could perpetrate the unthinkable and consign us along with the English, the Dutch and the Egyptians to the islands of Sicily and Sardinia.

Eventually, there were only two names left undrawn, Sweden and ourselves and the issue about to be resolved could scarcely be more stark. On the one hand, we could go in with Brazil, Scotland and Costa Rica at possibly two of the best venues in use, Turin and Genoa. The second prize was almost too bleak to contemplate. Brazil, the most magical name in football, held no particular fears for me. We had played them in Dublin in 1987 and made the broad world of

football sit up and take notice with a 1–0 win. Sure, the World Cup finals were different and apart from everything else, the Brazilians, loved by football crowds everywhere, would carry the neutral support. But that was a risk I was only too willing to take. Scotland, it scarcely needs saying, have never forgotten the night we surprised them in the European championship at Hampden Park. Andy Roxburgh, their manager, has never stopped telling me that the result would be different the next time we met—but then he would, wouldn't he? The Scots, for all the talent available to them, have never performed particularly well in the finals, however, and with the encouragement of that Hampden success behind us, I figured we could handle them. I sat there, almost too nervous to move, but hoping against hope, that ours would be the next name out.

Daniel Passerella reached into the glass jar, handed the slip to Herr Blatter and the next word that escaped his lips fell like the clap of doom on everybody in the Burlington Hotel: Sweden.

Bloody hell! I couldn't believe what I was hearing. Were FIFA, the people primarily responsible for law and order in the game, about to throw the best set of supporters in the world—ours—in with the lunatic fringe of the English and Dutch followers. Only too true they were. And as Blatter went through the formality of calling out our name, my mind was already racing ahead to the likely scenario in Italy in the summer.

I don't know a lot about either Cagliari or Palermo at this stage but enough to realise that we have just been landed with the worst of all possible draws. For one thing, they are putting our people at risk in the company of some of the most dangerous supporters anywhere in the two smallest stadia in use for the championships.

We have already been warned that the humidity in Palermo, where we would play Holland and Egypt, was the highest in any of the World Cup cities. If any of us ever had any doubt about the job specifications which awaited us when we set down in Italy, this has settled it.

I remember only too well the afternoon in Gelsenkirchen when the Dutch beat us in the European championship. It was hot, oppressively hot, that day and how they made us suffer in the sun. We had played two hard games against England and the Soviet Union and I genuinely feared that the Dutch, with their own particular brand of football, would drag the last ounce of energy from our players.

Most other continental teams play the ball short in neat, tightly patterned moves and you can legislate for that. But Holland are different. They don't pass the ball in the accepted sense, they boot it. And by spreading the play across the width of the park, they extract a heavy price from players trying to close them down.

Our lads were magnificent in Gelsenkirchen—perhaps unlucky to lose—but coming off the pitch that day every one of them knew they had just been through a killer of a game. It was an experience which I didn't wish to have repeated. And yet, here we were again, getting ready to go in against the Dutch.

As European champions, they didn't always play to their full potential in the qualifying rounds of the championship. But approaching the draw in Rome, I would have rated them as favourites to win the trophy.

At this point, of course, we aren't sure if they will have Ruud Gullit in their team in Italy. He has had a lot of injury problems in 1989 but it still hasn't prevented him from being named as World Player of the Year. It was an award with which I agreed for when Gullit puts it all together, it is almost impossible for a defender to stop him.

Then there is Marco Van Basten, another marvellous striker whose goal against the Soviet Union in the European final in Munich deserves to rate among the best ever scored at this level of competition. Together with Ronald Koeman, this pair give Holland a base which is the envy of every team in the world.

The incredible thing about the draw was that it not only lumps us with two of the countries we met in the Euro finals but in precisely the same order. Just as in West Germany we will start against England and finish our three-match qualifying programme against the Dutch. Substitute Egypt for the Soviet Union in the middle match and we are talking about exactly the same schedule.

In Stuttgart two years ago, we had put one over on the English by hitting them with an early goal and then defending with such discipline, that for all the pressure, they couldn't break us down in the second half. That was probably one of the Republic of Ireland's finest ever wins and in common with every Irish supporter, I realised then that it would be a hard act to follow. I have sufficient faith in my squad, however, to know that it can be done. Even as I looked up at the television screen in front of me, I wondered about the thoughts which would be running through Bobby Robson's mind at that moment—the more so since we are due to play England in a World Cup warm-up game in Dublin on 28 March.

When they eventually finished the draw, my initial fears were not for my players or, indeed, myself but for our supporters who were planning to travel with us to Italy. In all my years in the game I have never known a more loyal or better behaved set of fans and it annoys me intensely that, in a sense, they are now being thrown to the wolves. I am aware of how much they are looking forward to watching Ireland play in the finals and the financial sacrifices they will have to make to get there. Now, at a stroke, the hopes of some of those supporters have been destroyed.

Television pictures over the years have shown us just how volatile some of the English and Dutch supporters can be. It is apparent to me that many respectable people, appalled by any kind of violence at football games, will now be scared off by the memories of those pictures. Then there is the cost factor. A lot of those fans would, ordinarily, have been put to the pin of their collar to get the money together to go to Italy. Many of them have accompanied us on one or more of our overseas trips in the qualifying rounds and that added up to a lot of expense.

Now, instead of being settled in one of the mainland Italian cities, they are going to be put to additional expense in getting to the islands. That doesn't seem fair to me but then big business in the form of World Cup football doesn't always measure up on that score.

I felt like a drink. Together with John Givens, Trevor O'Rourke and a few others, I went back to my room as much to collect my thoughts as to wet my whistle. I had been there an hour or so when somebody came across to tell me that there was a phone call on the line from Rome. Bobby Robson, as I thought he might do, wanted to make contact with me. Bobby, more than most, has known the pressures of the management side of international football and I could well imagine him having to answer all those devious and, occasionally, stupid questions from journalists in Rome for the draw.

His first remark was: 'Here we go again, Jack—I don't think they did either of us any favours with that kind of draw.'

No less than me, he didn't want the Dutch and I had a sneaking feeling that he didn't want us either. Within a matter of seconds, he had got round to talking about the friendly game in March and the feasibility of going ahead with it. I had pencilled in the match as an important part of our Italian preparations. The sight of an England shirt always seems to bring out the best in the Irish and with both of us on a 'high', what better way to gear up for the finals?

Apart from that, there was a lot of money riding on the game. If we had the facilities, we could pack in a crowd of 100,000 for an England match. But even with an attendance ceiling of 50,000, the FAI still stood to make a lot of money. That was the positive side. On the other hand, we had to take account of the thugs who would almost certainly travel from England and the threat they posed to law and order in Dublin on the day of the game.

A one-off friendly game was fine but now that the countries were to meet again in Italy, the picture has changed totally. If, by chance, the rival fans got involved in Dublin, it might leave a residue of bad feeling which could spill over in Sardinia. It was a risk which neither of us could afford to take. So we contacted our respective governing bodies. Both the FA in London and the FAI in Dublin agreed to leave the decision up to Bobby and myself and pretty soon it became clear that we were both of the same mind on the matter. The Under-23 meeting of the countries can go ahead as scheduled but, reluctantly, there is no way that the senior game will be allowed to take place. That is an additional tab which we will have to pick up for the insensitivity of the FIFA people in Rome and it leaves us with a lot of difficulties in arranging an alternative game for 28 March.

I had not eaten all day and late in the evening we decided we would go down town to assess the reaction of people to the draw. We eventually stopped at a pub in Dorset St, a place I remembered well as the first pub I visited when I came with Leeds United to Dublin many years ago. What I didn't realise was that the clientele had changed totally and that it was now

something of an 'in' place for young people. The place came to a standstill when we arrived and I eventually ended up with two bodyguards around me.

It was evident from the conversation that these youngsters were every bit as disappointed as I was with the way the draw had worked out. The difference was that they had put it to the back of their minds and were now out to enjoy themselves. I thought to myself that there was a lesson there for me.

We stayed an hour or so and then, on the advice of Trevor O'Rourke, stopped off at what he called a GAA pub, The Hill 16 in Summerhill. I am never sure on these matters but, according to him, it would be an interesting place to test the water. No less than the last premises we visited, the mood there, among the football people, was one of disappointment and, in some cases, anger. They were perfectly prepared to see Ireland go in against Brazil, Argentina or even West Germany, but the prospect of a repeat of the European championships didn't particularly appeal to them. At least some of them voiced the misgivings which I had earlier in the day, that the extra expense of getting to Sicily and Sardinia would mean a change of plans for a sizeable section of those who had planned to travel. And the first edition of the Sunday papers confirmed that travel agents around the country shared those fears.

It was, then, a disastrous draw for everybody concerned but damn it, it's only a bloody game. We stayed there for an hour or more, got involved in a smashing sing-song and before leaving, we even persuaded them to put a picture of the Irish team in the bar. That was about the only win we had all day.

It was approximately one in the morning by the time we made it back to our hotel and, come to think of it, I never did get that meal. But, believe me, there was plenty of food for thought when I eventually got to bed!

JANUARY
1990

●

I've always enjoyed talking in public on my favourite subject, football. I like to speak my mind and respond as fairly and as factually as I can on those occasions when there is a question-and-answer session. But the Irish have long memories and because of that, I've had to deal with more questions on my relationship with Liam Brady and David O'Leary than almost any other topic during my public-speaking appearances in the last six months or so. Apart from the issue of how we would do when we got to Italy, I found myself explaining the situation of Brady and O'Leary at almost every one of those sessions. For me, both matters were rooted in history.

Liam Brady was given the chance to play his way into the squad for Italy and failed. Many of his supporters were, it seemed, unable or unwilling to accept that. The problem, as I saw it, was that these people remember Brady for what he had been. Sadly, however, the great days for Liam are only a memory now. And current

form is the only criterion I can use in selecting my team.

The case of David O'Leary is different. O'Leary was in the first Irish team I managed against Wales in March 1986 but did not play again for us until the meeting with Spain in Seville in November 1988. A lot of people will tell you that David was one of the best centre backs in British club football in that period and the word was that I wouldn't select him because we had fallen out. O'Leary, like Brady, was supposed to be at my throat and I even heard one story that we had a row at a football function in London. Well, I can tell you that the 'row' in London never took place. And there is certainly no player at my throat. The O'Leary saga lasted for almost three years—this is where the long memories came in—but I'm afraid the facts became a little distorted with the passage of time. Some journalists didn't help matters with articles they wrote. Players and journalists occasionally read into situations things that were never intended. And I recall sports writers making some play out of an incident at Parkhead in Glasgow.

Arsenal were playing Celtic in a friendly game and I had made the journey primarily to check on the fitness of Mick McCarthy. I went around to the players' room after the game and the first person I bumped into, coincidentally, was O'Leary. We spoke for a time but when McCarthy came out I left David and went across to Mick. This was apparently interpreted as a snub to David. There were even some journalists who cited it as an illustration that I didn't really like him.

That, of course, is rubbish. Personal likes or dislikes ought not enter into football management and they certainly don't with me. You pick the best available and to hell with the prejudices!

But the point people forget is that when you go to do your job and meet players after a game, there is only so much time for chat before everybody disappears. As I said, I went to look at McCarthy in particular but I also wanted to have a few words with Packie Bonner, Chris Morris and Celtic's manager, Billy McNeill who, after all, was providing me with three members of my squad.

If David O'Leary felt that I was deliberately chopping him off when I went to McCarthy, he obviously failed to take account of those restrictions.

There was, however, another incident which had a lot more relevance to O'Leary's international career and it happened a couple of months after I took over as manager. No disrespect to anybody, but the organisation at the FAI wasn't the best at the time. We had just played Wales but nobody appeared to have the slightest idea as to where we were going next.

I remember meeting Franz Beckenbauer, the West German manager, at a game in Europe in or around that time and he asked me what I had planned for our end-of-season programme. I told him that there was a possibility we might be playing in South America, that the possibility of a tour of Scandinavia had also been mentioned and there was even a chance that we might end up playing in a tournament in Iceland. Franz couldn't

believe it. 'We in West Germany', he told me, 'know precisely where we will be in the year 2000.'

I relate that merely to emphasise the uncertainty of the whole set-up in Ireland. I was not only in the position of being unable to alert my players for a call-up, I didn't even know where we might be playing in May—that was, if we played at all. Eventually, it was confirmed that we were playing in a three-nation tournament involving Iceland and Czechoslovakia in Reykjavik. But when I rang around to check on the availability of players, I discovered that some of them would not be in a position to join us.

I didn't include O'Leary in the original squad but that was my prerogative as manager. When one of the centre backs in the squad later withdrew, however, I contacted the Arsenal player and invited him to travel. He told me that he couldn't because he had arranged to take his family on holiday at the time of the tournament. I asked him to postpone the holiday but he said that it was out of the question. Fair enough. But we went on to win the tournament and David O'Leary couldn't blame me for the fact that other players proceeded to stake compelling claims for the two positions in central defence.

In addition to Mick McCarthy and Kevin Moran, I also had Mark Lawrenson and Paul McGrath available for the positions. Any two of them were capable of forming a partnership which would be the envy of many countries across the world. But many people in Ireland, including the football writers, couldn't or wouldn't accept that situation. They wanted O'Leary in the team at any price. What they refused to acknowledge was that he could only be accommodated at the expense of another player. And with four people capable of doing his job already in the squad, I often wondered just how many centre backs they wanted me to select.

I never doubted David's ability as a player. But if I'm honest, I must admit that I always had doubts about our ability to settle him into the side as it was beginning to develop. He is primarily a drop-off player at Arsenal where Tony Adams makes the first contact and O'Leary fills the hole at the back.

Our system is different. We require both our centre backs to get forward and make contact with the people in front of them. The ball which drops behind them then becomes the responsibility of the goalkeeper. When O'Leary eventually came back into the side in Seville in 1988, I called him up to my room and told him what we were about. To his credit, he has responded well with only the occasional exception—like the Spanish game in Dublin—but it pleases me that he is now an established member of the squad.

I say it again for it probably needs repetition to convince the doubters. I never had any feud with the lad. He was never at any stage excluded from my plans and I always maintained that when the need arose, I would be happy to have him back in my side. That fact recorded, I must put it on record that I was determined that I wouldn't be railroaded by anybody into playing him when I didn't consider that he would enhance the team at that particular time. This was a lesson I learned

a long time ago, from a remarkable man—Alf Ramsey.

The popular conception of Ramsey was of an aloof, slightly severe man and having played for him for six years, I must say that I couldn't totally disagree. Alf was certainly not the most approachable of men—not in my case, anyway—and if you had a problem, you tended to go elsewhere for advice.

Most people would interpret that as a minus but for all the gap in communications, his sense of presence was enormous. He didn't say much but we soon discovered that he didn't have to. He was the boss and we all knew it.

He was also one of the most single-minded men I have known. He knew exactly what he wanted and how he would set out to achieve it. Nothing, bar nothing, was allowed to stand in the way of bringing his dreams to fulfilment.

Even today, there are those who question his legacy to British football. England may have won the World Cup for the one and only time in 1966, but to some, success was achieved at a high price. Alf played without specialist wingers and for a generation which had grown up with players of the stature of Stanley Matthews and Tom Finney, that was hard to accept. The truth, of course, was that the game was evolving all the time and Ramsey was responding to the needs of the '60s. The monument to his career is that he got in first and imposed his strategy on others at a time when they hadn't yet learned how to counter it.

He was also among the first in the world to prove that the best eleven individuals do not, necessarily, make up into the best team. That philosophy is fairly common now but thirty years ago, it was still pretty innovative. It stood Ramsey and England in good stead. And it's my philosophy now.

Ramsey was, above all else, a man for the system. And, unashamedly, he picked the players to fit that system, irrespective of how they ranked with the public as individuals. In time, it produced some odd selections. The team plan was paramount to everything else and even if it meant the inclusion of players who might never, otherwise, have worn an England shirt, it stuck solid. Nobby Stiles was a case in point. That may sound like heresy to Nobby's many fans, particularly those who made him something of a cult figure at Manchester United, and I'm the first to hold up my hand and say that there was no braver or more loyal teammate anywhere. When it came to the more artistic side of the game, however, Norbert was not the kind of bloke to stand out in a crowd.

Alf had such a player in my brother Bobby. But in his case, he wasn't particularly clever in competing for and winning the ball. The younger Charlton was far too good to leave out, however, and Alf was able to accommodate him only by selecting Stiles. He now had two excellent players in their own right, one to get the ball and give it to the other who could use it. In those days, it was a novel way of putting a team together but it worked. I've never forgotten that lesson and the wisdom of using players who complement each other.

Long before we arrived at Wembley for the World Cup, Alf had done his homework and that, too, impressed me. With the exception of naming two strikers from three, Jimmy Greaves, Roger Hunt and Geoff Hurst, he knew exactly the team he wanted to play and, of course, he had that problem solved for him when Greaves got injured in the first game.

Which brings me back to Brady and O'Leary. My responsibility is to the general public. They don't turn up in droves at Lansdowne Road just to see Liam Brady or David O'Leary play. They want to see Ireland win. And it's my duty as team manager to do everything possible to deliver that result to them. If I were to sit and worry how players might react when they are left out of the side, I'd never get the job done. And in fairness, footballers, as a breed, accept that situation. After all, Gerry Daly came and went without any aggravation. Ashley Grimes did the same and the lad, Kelham O'Hanlon from Rotherham, has been with us on several occasions without ever getting a competitive game. That is the essence of the squad system. And once you explain your reasons for a decision to the players involved, you owe nobody any apologies. From my travels around Britain and Ireland, I believe the supporters understand the logic of that policy. And I've discovered that those people are very often more in touch with what is happening than some of the professionals.

EARLY FEBRUARY
1990

●

People are inevitably curious about my philosophy on the game. Over a period of almost 40 years either playing or watching football, certain points have made an indelible impression on my mind and, summarised, they go like this.

Never play the game the way the opposition have prepared for you to play it. Go out and do what they don't like.

During the World Cup finals in Mexico in '86, I watched all the great footballing nations in action and it struck me that, with one or two variations, they all played the same. They built their game skilfully and methodically from the back and in short, tightly patterned moves, they pushed the ball through the field.

There was no point in us trying to follow them and beat them at their own game for they had a ten-year start. So instead of attempting to play the ball through them, I decided we would go over them. And it worked.

Northampton on a wet Saturday in January is a long way removed from the environment of Mexico City but years earlier, I had seen the same basic logic in operation in the humble surrounds of the English Fourth Division championship. Northampton had devised a plan by which their outfield players had five seconds to get to the halfway line for a long kick out by their goalkeeper. When the ball dropped, they had invariably more players in the other half of the pitch than the opposition and by heading it on, they

were then in the position to trade on percentages. They won the championship by a mile.

The same fundamental logic of shunning the obvious, imposing the unexpected on the opposition and making them play the type of game that suits you applies to every level of football.

This sort of philosophy has been a long time in the making. Even as a young player, I had been preparing for a future career in management. For that, I can thank two men in particular, George Ainsley and Jimmy Frew. George was a Football Association coach, Jimmy worked as the area representative in Leeds and between them, they convinced me of the wisdom of doing the course for an FA preliminary coaching badge when I was still only 22.

That went against the norm for young players in that era but for me, it was one of the best moves I ever made. Before long, I was coaching in the local schools, often doing an hour-long session before reporting for training at Elland Road. Killing free time is often a tricky exercise for young professional players. But while many of them were hanging around bookmakers' offices and drinking coffee—I did a bit of that, too—I was out and about coaching boys and making myself some extra money. I was getting thirty old shillings (£1.50) for a session and at a time when I was earning somewhere between £17 and £20 a week at Leeds, a monthly cheque of £30 or £40 was very welcome indeed to a man with a young family. Apart from the money, the experience of getting up on your feet and addressing people was invaluable. After that, I went to Lilleshall to get my full coaching badge and that was a real eye-opener for me.

The players' course was held in conjunction with the managers' and trainers' programme and we got to work with people like Bill Shankley and Joe Mercer. Among the players who attended Lilleshall with me were Bobby Robson, Terry Veneables, Don Howe and Lawrie McMenamy and it was no coincidence that all four went on and distinguished themselves in management.

Walter Winterbottom was in charge at Lilleshall at the time and when Allen Wade took over, he invited me to travel down and supervise some of the preliminary badge courses. So at a stage when I was still only a young player, I was already on my way as a coach. When you are in charge of a course, it's your ideas people want to hear and it's your challenge to get the message across. Above all else, it gets you in front of people, talking, and that is where so many great players have failed as managers. For all their skills on the pitch, some players are incapable of explaining to an audience why an idea will or will not work. And that is down to the fact that, unlike us, they haven't been through the mill at Lilleshall. In a roundabout way, it also answers the question of why my brother Bobby never became a successful manager.

At Lilleshall, you found out pretty quickly about the strategies of football and the way the game was evolving. You learned, for example, how teams set about playing other sides and why. Things like that expanded your horizons. Everybody was

familiar with the problems at his own club but by mixing with others, you discovered what was happening around the country and got to be able to talk about arranging contracts and other relevant matters. In the end, it all gelled into making you a coach.

It did have a downside in so far as you did not accept decisions lightly when you went back to your own club. Billy Bremner may have been the team captain at Leeds but I quickly got a reputation as the talker. If we were discussing a particular point in training, I would always say my piece if I felt that it needed saying. Some of my teammates didn't take too kindly to that at times but I think Don Revie understood.

Ever since, I've been sold on the idea of players going to do the course at Lilleshall. It's not just a matter of what you learn but you get to meet people in the game who will, at a later stage, keep you in the game. For all the world, it's like a private members' club. I certainly would not employ anybody who hadn't been through the FA coaching course and it accounts directly, for what I consider the perfect working relationship with my assistant, Maurice Setters.

It was at Lilleshall that I first met Maurice and his name came instantly to mind when I needed a coach at Sheffield Wednesday. He was a colleague of Bobby's at Manchester United and we occasionally drank a pint together, when I got over there. That, I hasten to add, was not the reason I invited him to join me at Sheffield. I recognised in him the astute qualities which were essential to the job

I wanted him to do for me and, having parted company with Doncaster Rovers some time earlier, he was available.

Wednesday were close to the foot of the Third Division championship table at the time and I remember telling him that we didn't have an awful lot of cash to spend. Luckily, money wasn't the bottom line for either of us and thus began a partnership which was to grow into one of the happiest in the business.

An important part of the survival kit in his job is a capacity for watching a lot of football and I can think of nobody who sees more games than Maurice. And because of that, he is more in touch with what happens in the Midlands than the vast majority of other coaches. In fact, one of the biggest mistakes Newcastle made was in allowing him to leave after I had quit. Living in the north east of England, I was very much out on a limb whereas Maurice had his finger on the pulse over a much wider area.

Newcastle's loss was Ireland's gain and today the FAI is reaping the benefits which, with greater prudence, the top brass at St James's Park might be enjoying. Contrary to what many might believe, Maurice and I don't spend all our time watching the glamour games in England and Scotland. There is no point in either of us going to watch the Ronnie Whelans, Paul McGraths or Tony Cascarinos, apart from checking on fitness. We already know what they can do. The name of the game is to get out and look at younger, lesser-known players, people who have been recommended to us as potential internationals qualified to represent the Republic of Ireland. It can be long, tedious work but it has certainly paid off for us with the acquisition of players like Ray Houghton, John Aldridge and Andy Townsend.

That is why I am amused when I read that Andy Roxburgh, the Scottish manager, has complained that I have offered Bernie Slaven a place in the squad for the Welsh game in March. Andy is aggrieved that I have told Bernie, who was also qualified to play for Scotland, that he is in line for a call-up, seven weeks before the game. To me, that is rubbish. This has been no spur-of-the-moment decision, designed to tie Slaven to Ireland. Maurice and I have been watching him for months, weighing up the pros and cons before deciding that he was the right player for us. Scotland never once showed an interest in him until we moved. Or if they did, they kept very quiet about it.

Some people in football have never forgiven us for getting out and signing up players who were also qualified for other countries and who later developed into key members of the Ireland team. That is why I have found it necessary to be as discreet as possible when I go to a game to watch a potential Ireland player. Journalists occasionally accuse me of playing it too close to my chest and not informing them of any leads I might be following. If I do that, however, it alerts every other national team manager and, sure as hell, they'll move to cover themselves and, if possible, persuade the player to keep his options open. So, I keep my thoughts to myself.

FRIDAY 23 FEBRUARY
1990

●

Almost from the day he accepted the England post, Bobby Robson has been under the whip to produce. The fact that he has been responsible for far more good performances than bad ones hasn't really counted with his critics. They still want his scalp.

Managing England has, I suppose, always been like this. There is a sense of expectation among English people which is unmatched even among Italians, Germans or Brazilians that the country will be successful in football. Very often, those expectations are divorced from reality and the end-product is a lot of hassle, largely unjustified, for the manager and players of the day. And most of that hassle comes from the press.

I am reminded of this by a story in one of today's more lurid tabloids which has an unmerciful 'go' at Bobby for weaknesses which, in the opinion of the journalist, merit the sack for Robson.

Knocking the press is a practice which never fails to raise hackles of journalists. To put it mildly, that is ironic when you consider the amount of knocking they do in every facet of life, from football to politics. It simply has to be said that the sporting press has been culpable, in part, for the abnormal and unjustified pressure which has built up around consecutive England teams and their managers over the last twenty years.

To them, it is all a bit of a media game. They build personalities with fulsome praise and then chop them down, it seems to me, with even more relish. As far as they are concerned, everybody in the public eye is fair game. The truth is that they are less concerned with the manner in which the incumbent manager is making out than in speculating on his successor and where he will come from. They love to write, for instance, about Brian Clough but sure as hell, they'll be after him as well, if he ever gets the England job.

I don't deny that the press has an important job in the development and marketing of the game. But a section of the tabloid press, the biggest sellers, needs to examine its conscience on the way it is discharging that responsibility. Truth and honesty don't seem to matter with them. They'll shift their ground from one day to the next: angle their stories in whatever way suits their purpose and damn the consequences.

Bobby Robson can never win in those circumstances. If England come out on top in any particular game, they generally regard it as no more than the fulfilment of destiny. If the team loses, Robson will be crucified. I've had my differences with the people in charge of English football and how they run it. But I'll say this for the FA. They are deserving of our admiration for standing up to the press and refusing to be stampeded into sacking Bobby. Every team, from schoolboy to international level, needs stability. Without it, it is impossible to function efficiently. After all, there is not much point planning for next month if you're going to be fired next week.

It is fundamentally wrong for commentators to promote a climate of change for the sake of change. To do so is to undermine confidence and confidence derives from stability. That is why the FA, for all its faults, earns big credit marks for not listening to the rantings of some reporters. The day they yield to that pressure, they will turn a difficult job into an impossible one and render the managership of the England team virtually untenable.

If the football writers are really serious in their crusade to root out the evils of the British game and bring it to a position where it can trade at parity with the rest of the world, may I suggest that they look again at the structure of club football in England?

There are those who take pride in the fact that the Football League is probably the most competitive in the world. The Italians and the West Germans may look at it differently but in their heart of hearts, I feel that they, too, will acknowledge the unique make-up of the game in England. This has been reflected in a number of ways, not least in the outstanding record of English clubs in European competitions until their expulsion in the wake of Heysel. For all the glamour of the big continental clubs, there is little doubt that the three European club tournaments have been seriously devalued by the absence of the Liverpools, Arsenals, Evertons and so on.

From the standpoint of international team managers, the loss has also been substantial. Unlike the old days when people learned their trade with their clubs, newcomers to international football have now little or no idea of how to cope with Continental opponents. And that is a serious handicap. At club level, then, England can still look the world in the eye but those in authority have a stark choice to make. They can either go on overseeing the strongest league in the world or restructure the format to ensure that the country is represented properly in the major international competitions. They simply cannot have it both ways.

Take our preparations for international games. With rare exceptions, there is a full club programme the weekend before a Wednesday international fixture and that puts players at unnecessary risk.

A manager may have a huge squad but, invariably, he knows the team he wants to play in the approach to a game. If he loses two or three players before it—and this happens all the time to Robson and me—it destroys match strategy. You may bring in good-class replacements but the balance of the team is still undone. You hope and pray that it will work out on the day but that is not good enough for an important match.

Occasionally, the Football League authorities will postpone the Saturday programme as a big favour—but never for a 'friendly' game. That annoys me intensely. There is no such thing in the modern football calendar as a 'friendly' fixture. These games form a manager's preparation for the next competitive fixture and, as such, are vitally important. Unfortunately, they are never likely to be viewed as such by the clubs. And they will go on objecting to postponements for the very good reason that they are under intense pressure, financially. They must play to pay the bills and that is another indictment of the system. Clubs, it seems to me, will never have enough money. The more cash that comes into football, the more is spent on wages and transfers. At different times, the game in England has been subsidised by pools money, sponsorship and television fees but it still doesn't seem to make the slightest difference.

It's not for me to say that wages and transfer fees are too high but at some point, the finances of the game must be put on a basis whereby expenditure relates to direct income at the turnstiles. As it is, clubs must play twice a week to make ends meet. That is putting far too much pressure not just on players but on those international managers who are expected to turn out teams which will do their country proud.

Ideally, there should be no club demands on players for ten days before an international game. They should be allowed to rest for five or six days to recover from injury or fatigue, only reporting for duty the weekend before a game. It will require a revolution in thinking to bring it about but it is the only sure way forward.

I honestly believe that England have the potential to win the World Cup. But they'll do so only when they decide that they really want to win it.

That is why Bobby Robson has one of the most unenviable jobs in football. He is at the mercy of the system without the power

to change it. I wish some of his critics would remember that from time to time.

Making allowances for all that, I believe that Bobby has done reasonably well for England. He works hard, knows what he is about and his achievement in qualifying his team for the finals of the World Cup and European championship should not be underestimated.

I don't think England or Bobby got the credit they deserved in Mexico in '86. As I read it, they weren't a million miles from beating Argentina in the quarter-finals and, of course, the Argentinians went on to win the trophy.

The tragedy is that Bobby Robson is being fettered by an antiquated system at a time when England has the potential to be the best in the world. Most international managers, I reckon, would concede that in John Barnes and Chris Waddle, Bobby has two of the most exciting wingers in the world. There would be considerable support, too, for Terry Butcher's claims for a place in any world XI. A couple of years ago, Peter Shilton and Bryan Robson would have been entitled to the same rating. Age has now taken the edge off their game but they are still exceptionally good players by any standard.

These five players ought to provide the base for a successful team and yet England perform only rarely like a team with the class to impose themselves on any opposition. You'll get any number of arguments as to why that should be but as I interpret it, they have never really harnessed their assets properly. More than that, their strengths have, in some cases, spawned weaknesses.

Take, for example, Bryan Robson. It would be impossible to produce a more convincing player to illustrate the best in British football than Bryan. He's skilful, he's strong, can attack or defend and he goes where it hurts. He is unquestionably the most complete player that England has produced in modern times. And yet, I wonder . . .

There are times, I think, when managers become too reliant on particular players—times when we fill in one or two names automatically and build the rest of the team around them. Bobby Robson would seem to have that kind of fixation about his namesake. In a sense, I can identify with his dilemma. When I select an Irish team, I tend to start with Ronnie Whelan and build from there. Ronnie is so good at so many things, that it would be impossible to visualise an Irish side without him. The difference is that while I can slot Whelan into any one of three or four places in the team, Bobby Robson appears to be obsessed with the idea that England without Bryan Robson in central midfield is not what England ought to be.

There is no doubt in my mind that Bryan is, or was, England's best midfielder by a mile. The problem is that they never tied down the other position in central midfield and that was due, in part, to the way the team pattern evolved.

Bryan Robson is a capable defender but he cannot be expected to do that job in a match plan in which he is required to get into the opposing penalty area and score. In that situation, the need is for a strong, defensively minded player to anchor the other place in central midfield but, incredibly, they have never succeeded in finding him.

They tried Glen Hoddle there but it didn't work because like Bryan, Hoddle wanted to get forward. Steve McMahon and Neil Webb were better suited to the job but as in the case of Peter Reid—and heaven knows, he was around long enough to know all the tricks of the trade—they never really established themselves as top-class internationals. Why? For the answer, I think we're back to the fact that Bobby Robson's assets have, in a sense, rebounded on him. Nobody will deny that Waddle and Barnes are exciting wingers but the reality is that they're not too clever when it comes to defending.

If you play Waddle and Barnes in the same side, you've got to man midfield in such a way that the gaps they leave behind them are filled. By detailing Bryan Robson to act as an extra forward, you merely compound the problem. That, in my opinion, is the real reason why an exeptionally fine club player like McMahon has never made it with England. Bobby Robson has simply thinned down midfield to the point where they are apt to be exposed by the quick break. Nobody, not even a grafter like McMahon, can be expected to cover right across midfield.

The gamble of playing two specialist wingers like Barnes and Waddle can, I believe, only be justified, by anchoring two players in midfield. It would mean sacrificing Bryan Robson's flair in the penalty area but that is an equation which Bobby Robson must work out for himself.

John Barnes enjoyed another magnificent season with Liverpool but I am not alone in thinking that England doesn't always get the best out of him. A player like Barnsey needs time and space to run at defenders. Unfortunately, the pace of the game England plays, with the emphasis on the slow, methodical build-up from midfield, doesn't always give him that opportunity.

Crowds love to see big, pacey wingers attacking full backs but the manner in which international football has developed means that the spectacle is becoming rarer and rarer. The Italians and the West Germans are past masters at getting players behind the ball and if a winger is lucky enough to beat his opponent, he will, invariably, find others queuing up to meet him.

The only answer is to spread the ball quickly to the flanks but too often Barnes and Waddle take man and ball together. Given the high price England must pay for including these two players, it's a fault which cries out for correction. The other point which has never ceased to baffle me about consecutive England teams is the uncertainty in the centre of their attack. I think Bobby has chopped and changed in these two positions more than in any other sector of the team. And it shows.

Gary Lineker is, or was a couple of years ago, one of the fastest strikers around, a point he illustrated time and again when we played England in the finals of the European championship in West Germany. But Bobby, it seems to me, has never been able to make up his mind firmly whether to use him as a target man or a runner. He has been used in both roles in different permutations with people like Peter Beardsley, Steve Bull and Nigel Clough but somehow it has never worked out quite to plan.

I believe that Gary is most useful to England as a runner but that entails finding an effective target man who can exploit his acceleration over ten or fifteen yards. The primary need is for a strong, accurate header of the ball but, as yet, nobody has stuck in this role. Lineker himself is reasonably good in the air but I don't think he could ever be classified as the type who dominates defenders and terrifies goalkeepers. Bobby has tried players who appeared to have the equipment to fill the bill, players like Ray Harford, but all to no avail. Given the fact that Barnes and Waddle are in the team primarily to get to the back line and cross the ball, that is as costly as it is surprising.

I like Terry Butcher. The lad is hard and competitive, wants to take charge of his penalty area and when the going gets tough he is never likely to go missing. It needs a certain type of player to complement someone like Butcher, however, and Robson hasn't always come up with the answer. Because of the defensive deficiencies of Barnes and Waddle, it has frequently been necessary to push the two full backs forward to plug the gaps and it is in this situation that the English are most vulnerable.

Teams prepared to have a go and run at England will continue to give them problems. Here's to 12 June!

TUESDAY 27
March 1990

●

Approaching tomorrow's game against Wales at Lansdowne Road, I am faced with something of a crisis of priorities. We are less than three months away from the World Cup finals and the hype is growing by the day. The match will attract anything up to 45,000 spectators. And when that many people turn up at a stadium, I like to give them what they want—a win.

The fans apart, there are other compelling reasons to give the game everything we've got. We are on a good streak and football people will tell you that there is nothing to boost a team's confidence like a long run of success. Against that, however, I have to balance the need to try out a few things to assist me in the task of naming the 22 players I will take to Italy. After giving it a lot of thought, I am going for the second option.

In fact, my hand was forced to some degree by the fact that John Aldridge had gone and done his shoulder in Spain and Ray Houghton, of course, is ruled out because of a one-match suspension. Ray was booked twice in the World Cup qualifying games and FIFA, to our relief, ruled that the ensuing ban could be applied to a friendly game rather than in the finals. I thought that most football people in the country were familiar with that saga—but not, apparently, the man, himself. When I announced my squad for the Welsh fixture, I had several irate calls from Liverpool, including one from Ray,

wondering why he had been left out! The FAI had sent me a copy of the FIFA notice confirming the suspension but nobody had seen fit to inform Houghton, presumably because they felt he already knew of it. Incredibly, he didn't—and in that he was probably in a minority of one.

Aldridge was no less disappointed in the fact that he wasn't coming to Dublin to join us but even if he had been fit, I wouldn't have played him. From a long way back, I had decided that this was the game in which I would introduce Bernie Slaven to the Irish public. Aldo had done a tremendous job for us as the 'runner' in the front line over the years but after the European championship finals I became increasingly aware that our cover in that role was, to say the least, sparse.

At that point, I must admit that I was disappointed with the way that David Kelly's career had deteriorated. When I first saw him at Walsall, he looked a smashing prospect and he confirmed it by hitting three goals on his first international appearance against Israel at Dalymount. His was a talent which deserved the stage of First Division football but the move, when it came, nearly ruined him. For some strange reason, he never really hit it off with West Ham and his career was beginning to fall apart.

But football, as Jimmy Greaves is apt to say, is a funny old game and two developments are helping to get David back on the rails. First, he has transferred to Leicester City, a move which at the time may not have looked particularly clever but which I think is one of the best things he ever did. Then there was today's 'B'

△ Tony Cascarino beats Andy Melville of Wales.

△ Russia's Tishenko caught between Gary Waddock and Paul McGrath.

The last farewell for one of the greats. Liam Brady at his testimonial match against Finland at Lansdowne Road in May, our last home game before Italy.

international game against England at Cork where he covered himself in glory in a superb 4–1 win. But, to be honest, he wasn't in the 'frame' when I chose the squad for the Welsh fixture.

Perry Groves of Arsenal whom Maurice Setters and I had watched on a number of occasions, is another striker who has figured in our thoughts. George Graham rates him fairly highly but he doesn't appeal to me as a player who will strengthen our squad at this particular time.

Slaven is different. He has come up the hard way, knows how to look after himself now that he has eventually made it with Middlesbrough and, generally, he fits the description of a good professional. At 29, he is no spring chicken but that doesn't bother me too much. I need somebody who can contribute to the squad in Italy—and I need him fast. We had been watching Bernie for a long time before we popped the question and the answer was as expected. Sure, he'd love to play for Ireland. I was quite specific when I spoke to him about the job opportunities. I told him that there were no guarantees he would be in our World Cup squad but if he did the business, he could expect to be part of the Irish scene for the next two or three years. He was happy to go with that challenge and once the requisite paperwork had been done, I told him that he could expect to pull on a green shirt for the first time against Wales.

Bernie, of course, was born in Glasgow of Irish parentage and, inevitably, the news that he was coming to play for us moved the cynics to suggest yet again that we should call our team the League of Nations. Ever since we began to get a little success, they have been sniping at us but that, in a way, is proof that we are beginning to come of age. People of that particular breed don't tend to notice you when you're down on your luck.

I owed and owe nobody any apology for the players I pick. I have never, for example, stepped outside the eligibility rules laid down by FIFA when inviting people to play for us. They may not all have been born in Ireland but they had their roots in the country. Had economic circumstances not forced their ancestors to emigrate, they would have grown up and worked in Ireland. The fact that it didn't work out like that made them no less Irish. True, the accents in our dressing room tend to vary a little. But, believe me, once these fellows don the green, they would run through a brick wall to get a good result for Ireland. I think people like Mick McCarthy, Ray Houghton, John Aldridge and Chris Hughton have made that point over and over again.

All right, we take advantage of the ancestry rule to build our squad but so, too, do other countries around the world. You don't find too many English critics pinpointing the case of John Barnes for instance.

John Byrne and John Sheridan are two other members of our squad who first saw the light of day in England and I have decided that both should be given the chance of proving what they can do in this particular game.

Byrne has been part of the squad ever since I became involved but he tended to be used mainly as a substitute. He has now developed as a right-sided midfield player with Le Havre in France and with Houghton unavailable, this seems the ideal opportunity to see what he can do over the full ninety minutes.

Sheridan is a bit of an enigma. When he does things well, he is in a class of his own—a magnificent striker of the ball who can lift a crowd with just one sliderule pass. Against that, however, he has some infuriating weaknesses which so far, have defied all advice.

He hadn't played for us since that miserable night in Seville almost 18 months ago when he suffered almost as much as I did in the 2–0 defeat by Spain. In fairness, we weren't the only ones who wished they were somewhere else that night. That, I felt, wasn't the true John Sheridan and he deserved the chance of proving what he could do before we set off for the finals. It had been a long time since he was with us—so long, in fact, that he appeared to have forgotten the squad rules. He turned up at our hotel ninety minutes after the appointed time and I saw red. It wasn't the reception I had planned to give him but rules are rules. If I let that incident go without question, the whole system might have disintegrated around me.

I had intended to play Gerry Peyton against Wales but unfortunately he picked up an injury with Bournemouth last week. That was as untimely for me as it was for him for it robbed me of the chance of settling him back into the side. Paddy Bonner is, of course, our first choice goalkeeper but every so often, I break

out in a cold sweat when I picture the scenario of Packie getting injured before or during the World Cup finals. That is not to suggest that I don't have confidence in Peyton. But only those who have played in the position can fully appreciate how important it is for a central defender to be on the same wavelength as his 'keeper.

That kind of rapport can only be achieved over a period of time and while Gerry had been an essential part of our squad for many years, it worried me that he hadn't actually played in the team for some time. I didn't want to wait until we got into a fire brigade situation in Italy, to find out if he was in tune with his fellow defenders.

Sadly, that opportunity won't present itself for the Welsh game but at least I have the consolation of welcoming Mick McCarthy back to his old stomping ground in central defence. Mick joined Millwall from Olympique Lyons only last week after being out of first-team football for five months but I couldn't believe my eyes when I saw him. At a glance, it seemed to me that he had shed at least half a stone in his efforts to get match fit again. That, for me, is the mark of a true professional and it reflects the immense commitment of the man to be part of the cast in Italy.

Like Bernie Slaven, John Byrne and John Sheridan, he has to go into the side to meet Wales if only to prove that his movement has not been impaired by his long lay-off. The fact that Kevin Moran is joining him in the centre of the defence is an added bonus.

I announced the side early this morning and then dashed to Cork to see the 'B' international. This was to have been the curtain-raiser for the ill-fated senior fixture with England. That match was cancelled after the World Cup final draw—but was I glad they saved the 'B' game!

In short, this has been one of the most rewarding days since I teamed up with the FAI. Not merely did we win 4–1 but we achieved it in a manner which proved to me that we are headed in the right direction with the young talent which is beginning to come to the surface.

The scoreline was all the more remarkable because it appeared to be a mismatch. When the fixture was first mooted, I suggested to Bobby Robson that we confine it to players under 23. This was agreed with the proviso that we could use one or two players over the age limit to ensure that the game was competitive. Somewhere along the line, however, communications got fouled up and while we stuck to the terms of the original agreement, England ended up playing a senior team which, I venture to suggest, contained many of the players they will use in the 1992 European championship. In those circumstances, I reckoned we would do extremely well to get a draw. To win by three clear goals after going one down early in the game was an outstanding achievement.

After the game, some were unkind enough to carp about the conditions at Turner's Cross, explaining away the inept performances of many of the English players with the excuse that they couldn't perform on that kind of surface. To me and to many others, it just didn't wash.

The conditions were the same for both teams and our players were accustomed to performing on the same kind of pitches, week in, week out, as the England players. Moreover, the pitch, I thought, was acceptable. It was reasonably flat with a good covering of grass and, as such, was a fair test.

No, the result had less to do with the conditions than the fact that we played infinitely better on the day. Niall Quinn and David Kelly were tremendous, competing aggressively and giving Tony Adams and Andy Linighan the type of afternoon they will want to forget.

Ironically, a story had earlier appeared in the papers to the effect that we asked Linighan, a lad with Irish qualifications, to play for us. That was untrue. We did watch him on a couple of occasions but we never at any stage invited him to wear a green shirt. Andy is a good central defender who has produced some exciting displays for Norwich but on the evidence of what we saw in Cork, we already have better players in his position.

There were several exciting features to recommend the Irish team at Turner's Cross but the player who really took my eye was Alan McLoughlin of Swindon Town. Every so often, a gem appears to give managers new hope and for me, McLoughlin was that player. With so much pressure on to get good results, there have not been too many opportunities in the last two years to try out young players and in that situation, I have often worried how we would make out when the time came for some of our senior citizens to call it a day.

Fears like that made the trip to Cork all the more rewarding for me. McLoughlin was at Manchester United for a couple of years before joining Swindon and was recommended to me in the first instance by Tony Galvin. Alan joined us with the astonishing record of having scored 18 times from midfield for Swindon since the start of the season. Looking at him today, I understood why. He was alert and skilful, ran aggressively and, of course, he got the goal which hauled us back into the game.

There were several other success stories. Players like Brian Mooney and the Oldham pair, Denis Irwin and Mike Milligan, all did well, so if people notice an extra spring in my step this evening, it is understandable. We have gone and beaten an England team that was senior in everything but name—and we have done it with style.

The Welsh game, I fear, will be something else. In four previous meetings with them, Ireland has never won and despite the fact that Terry Yorath has had to replace Mark Hughes and Kevin Ratcliffe, I reckon that they will give us another tough game. Wales, of course, have failed to make the cut for the World Cup finals but that doesn't disguise the fact that when they get it right they are a match for any team.

Neville Southall, for instance, is a goalkeeper who could hold his own in any company and then there is Ian Rush. I still have painful memories of that moment when Rushie slipped our central defenders and headed the goal that turned my first assignment with the Irish team

into a 1–0 defeat some four years ago.

That was vintage Rush and I think all of us are now aware of the threat. After going through a sticky patch on his return to Liverpool from Juventus, Ian is beginning to play well again—well enough to present Mick McCarthy and Kevin Moran with the kind of examination that would search out any flaws in their game.

Rush, of course, is lining up against two of his Liverpool colleagues, Ronnie Whelan and Steve Staunton but if I'm honest, I've got to say that I don't want Whelan to play. He reported a slight groin strain when he joined us yesterday but still insisted that he be considered for selection.

That, it has to be said, is the mark of a good competitor but in this particular case, it irked me a bit. Ronnie has had a long, busy season with Liverpool and I feel that he could benefit from a little rest now and then.

The interests of international and club managers are often at odds but my advice to the Irish players in the approach to Italy is to pull out of club games if they feel the slightest twinge.

That, it could be argued, is cheating a little and if the roles were reversed and I were in Kenny Dalglish's position, I would be annoyed at the very suggestion. Looking at it from a purely selfish viewpoint, however, I reckon that a player would be better advised to miss a club fixture rather than risk aggravating an injury which could conceivably keep him out of the World Cup finals.

In Whelan's case, however, I am wasting my breath. Perhaps, it was the fear that he wouldn't get back into Liverpool's team if he dropped out—unjustified in my opinion—but he was adamant that he would make himself available for every fixture they played. He adopted the same attitude for the Wales game and, in the last analysis, I have to be influenced by his judgment, that his leg is strong enough to stand up to the test.

WEDNESDAY 28
March 1990

●

As soon as I turned up at Lansdowne Road, I knew that Whelan would struggle. For one thing, the pitch was bloody awful, hard and bumpy with not enough rain and very little grass to help the players. The surface there is always a bit dodgy for soccer in March but this was something else. That was only half the story. To the appalling ground conditions was added the hazard of a strong, gusting wind. Throw in the abrasive nature of all Welsh teams and you had the recipe for a wholly forgettable game. The good thing was that we won 1–0 and in so doing, stretched our unbeaten record in Dublin to 18 games. That, in anybody's language, is the badge of consistency.

It is fair to suggest that the number of good passes in the game could be counted on the fingers of one hand and all of them came from John Sheridan. But if the day lacked subtlety, it was still a hell of a game physically. That, as I saw it, was a useful bonus. We needed to play a British team before going in against England at Cagliari and if Wales scarcely possess the same degree of individual skill as the English it was still an important exercise.

We succeeded also in coping with the threat presented by Ian Rush. Apart from an isolated incident when he got away from Kevin Moran, he never really counted. And in that instance, the glancing header brought an equally good save from Paddy Bonner.

Southall, by comparison, was busy in the other goal and he showed yet again what a fine 'keeper he is with a remarkable save from Tony Cascarino early in the game. Tony was entitled to feel that he had done it all right with the firm, downward header from a cross by John Byrne. But Southall held the ball brilliantly. Cascarino moved just a few days ago from Millwall to Aston Villa for a fee of £1.5m and that added up to extra pressure for him. I thought he handled it well and was unlucky, yet again, not to have scored with a crashing header which came back off the crossbar.

Whelan, as I anticipated, didn't make it out for the second half and that gave me the chance of bringing Kevin Sheedy back into the team. There are few more composed or skilful players on the ball than Kevin and I think he proved it today by the way in which he brought some sense of order to an otherwise undistinguished game.

We were only four minutes away from the draw which, I thought, Wales had set out to achieve when Bernie Slaven pounced for the goal which he will treasure for the rest of his days. One of the things which had impressed me when I watched him at Middlesbrough was his perception and speed off the mark and they now came together to produce a dramatic winner. When Bonner's long clearance was knocked forward, Slaven was on to it like a flash and after taking the ball around Southall, he committed Gavin Maguire to the despairing handball stop on the line.

One of the downsides of my visit to Cork yesterday was that I couldn't take the team talk and in my absence the players agreed among themselves that if we got a penalty, Sheedy would take it. The logic of that decision left me cold for if there was one man who knew all about Kevin's penalty-taking technique, it was Neville Southall, his Everton clubmate who just happened to be keeping goal for Wales that day.

I closed my eyes as Kevin ran up to the ball and opened them again just in time to see the goalkeeper parry the shot to his right. The rebound would fall to the player who reacted fastest. Guess who got there first—Slaven! In that, there was an element of justice for I considered that he was unlucky not to have scored in the first place. I couldn't have been happier for him for he had undertaken a difficult test and done extremely well. I would like to have seen us with more possession in Wales's last third of the pitch to find out how he coped but as it was, I felt that he competed well, linked cleverly with Cascarino and showed that he was capable of holding the ball until the support arrived.

The other people on trial had games of varying quality. Byrne again showed excellent skill in getting away from his marker and occasionally sorted out the good pass. I must say, however, that he didn't impress me as a lad who would do a full 90-minute job for Ireland.

I've mentioned the fact that John Sheridan accounted for most of the telling passes that went in. John is good at that but on occasions such as this, I'm examining the negative as well as the positive and fuming over the things players are not doing.

I want to see them put their foot in, track, defend and, when the opportunity presents itself, get forward and support. In short, I'm looking for the total player, not just one who catches the eye in flashes. It's amazing how often people go along to a game and see only the flashy bits. A player may sweat his guts out in a grafting role for 90 minutes but it's a pound to a penny the spectators will come away remembering the guy who does something spectacular every twenty minutes or so. And it's not only the fans who err on this point.

In my early days at Leeds, I played all over the pitch, galloping up and down the park to join in set-piece moves. I scored a fair few goals in that time in addition to laying them on for others but, inevitably, there were occasions when the opposition broke back quickly and I was criticised for being caught out of position. So I went to Don Revie, told him I had enough of the hero bit and that in future, I was going to do only what I was paid to do—defend. I did and the result was that I was called up by England within a year. Naturally, I didn't feel like arguing the point at the time but that was rubbish. From a team point of view, I had been doing all the right things and only in some instances getting stick. Yet, when I opted out and settled just for defending, they gave me an England cap. That didn't and still doesn't make sense to me.

All that is by way of saying that I'm not totally happy with Sheridan's display against Wales, despite the fact that many people seem to think that he has had a good game.

These same people are lashing Chris Morris's performance at right back and again I think they are wrong. There were, of course, times when his crosses were off target but they seem to forget that Chris is primarily a defender. When he gets forward, as he often does, it's a bonus. Given the conditions and the speed at which he plays, it isn't the easiest job to cross accurately. The know-alls should try it some day.

Nor was I too disappointed with the performance of Andy Townsend in an unfamiliar role on the left side of midfield. He did the job I asked of him and on a better surface might have had more to show for his efforts.

With the winning goal coming so late in the game, the Welsh probably felt a little cheated and they knew for certain that they had been robbed when they got back to their dressing room and discovered that somebody had broken in. But that's another story . . .

SATURDAY 21
April 1990

●

There is some disturbing news today. Disturbing, that is, if you happen to be Irish, English or Egyptian but pretty reassuring if you support the Dutch national team.

Ruud Gullit has had a fitness test in Milan and the word is that he hopes to play for his club, AC Milan in their Italian championship game against Genoa tomorrow. It will be his first appearance for AC Milan in ten months. The plan is to have Gullit ready for the Italian Cup final against Juventus next Wednesday and then hopefully play him in the European Cup final in Vienna next month.

Gullit has had three operations on his knee and at one time it was feared that he might never play again. To that extent, I suppose, we should all be glad that the injury has responded to treatment and that people will have another opportunity to appreciate the skills which put him apart from most of his contemporaries. Still, it won't make our task at Palermo on 21 June any easier.

I remember Gullit well from Germany. He didn't have his greatest game against us and you can put that down to the way our defenders carried out their pre-match instructions to the letter. They sat on him throughout the full 90 minutes, closed him down so that he was never able to play the ball from the positions in which he wanted to play it and generally gave him as hard a game as he has ever endured in international football. The mark of the man, however, is that you can never be certain that you have put him out of a game completely. He may be shadowed successfully for 89 minutes but give him just one opening and he is capable of undoing everything you have achieved.

Gullit's on-going injury crisis is only one cloud on Holland's horizon. Another is the hassle which has resulted in the departure of their manager, Thijs Libregts, at a stage when he ought to have been firmly in control. Libregts did not appear to enjoy the confidence of some of his senior players. I don't pretend to know the inner politics of that situation but when a manager arrives at a point where he appears to be in basic conflict with his team, there is really no place for him to go.

Leo Beenhakker has inherited a team which, for all its extravagant talent, appears to be at odds with itself. The question is whether all this hassle will affect their performance in Italy. Only time will tell.

SUNDAY 22
April 1990

●

What a week! The mileage I clocked up was something else. I criss-crossed the country so often that at times, I was in danger of meeting myself coming back.

On Tuesday, I caught a plane from Newcastle to Dublin and then another to Cork to be there for a lunch-time engagement. That finished, I went by road to Waterford for a debate in the evening and then motored back to Dublin.

The next morning I was up early to catch a flight to Limerick, was back in Dublin by six o'clock and was off within the hour to another gig in Wicklow. Thursday saw me in Galway for lunch, in Athlone for another evening debate and then back in the car, heading for Dublin.

I had three engagements in the city on Friday, the last of them finishing at 1 a.m. I was up at six yesterday morning for the flight back to Newcastle, a quick wash and I was on my way to a game in the afternoon.

Workloads like that are no joke. Any money I get from the World Cup, I am earning. I have to get off my backside to go and do it and in that situation, there are no explanations owing to anybody. And while the work is exhausting, it is also very satisfying. It is remarkable to see the number of youngsters, from three years upwards, who turn out with flags and autograph books to see us. And I'm sure that, in time, it will be reflected in football taking deeper root in those areas in which it hadn't always been traditional.

Anyway, I'm doing all this with my eyes open. Twelve months ago I was faced with a choice. I could confine myself to football matters and my routine engagements in England and enjoy my days off, either fishing or shooting, or throw myself body and soul into the public-speaking circuit in Ireland and make hay while the sun shone. It meant that I could be away for five or six days at a time and that added up to a huge sacrifice in home life. Pat and I discussed it all at length and eventually we made our choice. It means a lot of long, lonely hours for her but we have decided to go with it. And for me, while I couldn't take too many weeks like last week, a lot of the time it is great fun.

TUESDAY 24
April 1990

●

The pitch at Lansdowne Road for tomorrow's game against Russia is a disgrace. I know that I had the same complaint before the Wales game but, to be fair, that was no more than I expected. Pitches in England in March are no great shakes but at least they are flat.

But when you arrive at the last week in April, you are entitled to find a well-grassed, rut-free surface which will give players a reasonable chance of expressing their skills. That is simply not the case in this instance.

The groundsman can scarcely be held responsible for the fact that the rainfall for April has been below average but the IRFU, the owners of the stadium, have aggravated the situation by allowing two rugby club games to be played here only three days ago.

Lansdowne is, of course, a rugby stadium and rugby people will probably be infuriated by the suggestion that these fixtures should be staged elsewhere. But the IRFU receives a lot of money for hiring the ground to the FAI and that must carry certain obligations. They have known for six months or more that the ground would be required for a football game on 25 April. In those circumstances,

it was incomprehensible that they should put the pitch at risk by insisting on going ahead with the club programme.

Unfortunately, it is a problem which is not going to go away for, barring the unforeseen, the FAI is unlikely to be able to fund the construction of a stadium of its own. Given the high profile of the national team and the upsurge of the game at all levels around the country, that is regrettable.

In every other respect, however, the FAI has made substantial advances. For one thing, the refurbishing of the Association's headquarters was a timely and well-advised move. When I first arrived in Dublin, I recall remarking that the building reflected no credit on anybody and there was, to put it kindly, a lack of urgency about the place.

Happily, all that has now changed. The FAI today operates from a modern, well-appointed complex and, more importantly, there is an element of efficiency there which, I like to think, reflects the new image of the national team.

A lot of the credit is down to Tony O'Neill who has streamlined the organisation to the point where if something needs to be done, it will be done without a second request. There ought to be credit, too, for the manner in which Donie Butler has revamped the marketing side of the operation. Thanks to his efforts, football has now developed a corporate image and this, allied to the traditional base, has brought new money into the game.

It doesn't need me to say that it hadn't always been so. Things were so dodgy back in 1985 that it was deemed necessary to devise a nation-wide fund-raising scheme to pump a few pounds into Irish football. Unfortunately, that scheme never got off the ground, due in part to the fact that certain journalists didn't want it to get off the ground. That dog-in-the-manger attitude infuriates me. So, these people didn't want the lottery to take place. Fine, but what counter-proposals did they come up with? None.

The end-product was that instead of funds being available to assist in the development of the national team, the whole process was reversed and the squad became the fund-raisers for the association. I am delighted that we were able to deliver but that added up to a lot of additional pressure for the players and myself.

WEDNESDAY 25
April 1990

●

You would need a sense of humour looking at the pitch for the Soviet game. What Valeri Lobanovsky, the Soviet manager, thought of it all, heaven knows but I think it is fair to say that he wasn't amused.

It's funny but people always seem to think that it is the visiting team which is handicapped most in such situations. In fact, the opposite is the case. When you favour a long ball type of game, as we do, you are heavily dependent on a true surface to offer a reasonable chance of a pass reaching its target.

The Soviets, by contrast, tend to play it short but as we discovered at Hanover

and again in Dublin, they are capable of producing the 35- or 40-yard pass which can rip open even the most vigilant defence.

Ever since our World Cup warm-up programme was finalised, I had identified this fixture as the one which would tell us what we needed to know in the approach to Italy. The Soviets are a good technical team who invariably compete well, home or away, and if there was one country capable of putting us to the test in Dublin, it was they.

In truth, it turned out to be something less than that. As soon as I saw their preliminary squad, I realised that Lobanovsky, shrewd as they come, had decided to keep some aces up his sleeve.

To be fair, his hand was forced to some degree. The days when all the star Soviet players stayed at home and the national team manager had his choice of what he wanted are gone. Now their better players are more often than not, to be found in Western Europe and Lobanovsky, like the rest of us, has to rely on the goodwill of club managers when he sets out to assemble a squad.

It accounted for the fact that players of the quality of Rinat Dasaev, Alexander Zavarov, Vladimir Bessonov and Segei Aleinikov were not in Dublin and to these were added the names of Vasily Rats, Alexei Mikhailichenko and Oleg Protassov, all injured.

This meant that the Soviets put a heavily improvised team in the field against us and the effect was to strip the game of much of its significance as a true World Cup test. In that situation, I have decided that I will again try a few things. Like Lobanovsky, I am working off a depleted squad. John Aldridge is club-tied in Spain and the Liverpool pair, Ray Houghton and Ronnie Whelan, are both injured.

The most maddening thing, however, is the refusal of Swindon Town and Middlesbrough to make Alan McLoughlin and Bernie Slaven available to us. Let me say at once that I have no axe to grind with either club. Both have a lot to fight for— Swindon to get out of the Second Division, Middlesbrough to stay in it—and in these circumstances, they have no desire to lose international players. A lot of hard work has gone into the season and nobody can point the finger at them for looking after their own interests. But it points up, yet again, the weaknesses of a League set-up in which Ireland, with no direct input into the administrative process, can be denied access to our players for all but three or four specified international dates.

In the case of Swindon, I understand that they had reached agreement with Newcastle to put back their game for a week but for some reason best known to themselves, the Football League authorities insisted that it should go ahead as scheduled. That was regrettable for it deprived McLoughlin of a precious chance to prove that he deserved a place among the 22 players going to the finals. Even before the Soviet game, I suspected that he would struggle to get a release for either the Finland or the Turkey game.

I feel sorry for the lad. He did all that was required of him in the 'B' international against England and is clearly a player of tremendous potential for Ireland. But for all his latent talent, the gamble of taking an uncapped player to Italy would be enormous. Much the same doubt attaches to Slaven. He did well on his debut against Wales but I would like to have seen how he made out against the cagey Soviet defence.

I haven't picked Frank Stapleton in the squad purely because there was no need to have him with us for this particular match. Frank has been around for a long time. I know exactly what he can do and there doesn't seem much point in selecting him at a time when I need to look at other, less experienced members of the squad.

Ironically, it is probably because of his vast experience and the fact that he is now coming to the end of his career that he feels so agitated about his chances of getting into the World Cup squad. Players read all kinds of things into situations and Frank has been so upset that he has gone public on the fact that I didn't phone him to tell him he was out of the squad.

That is true and I make no apology for it. I didn't contact John Aldridge either but he hasn't taken umbrage. The day that I have to start ringing around and telling them why I left them out is the day when I'll have to start worrying. International team managers invite players to come and represent their country. That is the beginning and end of it and there should be no obligation to apologise for leaving any player out.

I didn't select John Sheridan for the Soviet game but as it turned out, I had to get on to Sheffield Wednesday just a couple of days ago with an urgent request for him to travel to Dublin. At that stage, I was down to fourteen fit players but unfortunately John himself joined the casualty list on Saturday and was not permitted to travel.

I needed another midfield player in the squad and who better to do the job for me than Gary Waddock. He has just returned to Millwall's team after an absence of two weeks with a foot injury and as one of those pressing for a place in the squad going to Italy, he needs to show me that the lay-off has not affected his game.

I wasn't involved with the FAI when Waddock was playing regularly for Ireland but I recall him as a very useful member of QPR's team. At his best, he certainly has the potential to contribute to our plans.

One of the first things I did when the players arrived on Monday was to take Kevin Moran, Tony Cascarino and Paddy Bonner aside and tell them that they would be sitting on the bench. There was no hassle, no argument—I told them the reasons why and they accepted them.

I was still chewing over my permutation of centre backs for Italy and I needed all the evidence I could get to help me reach the right decision. Kevin and Mick McCarthy had started the game against Wales—now it is the turn of David O'Leary to go back into the team again and do his stuff.

Cascarino has had a long, punishing season at club and international level and he needs a short rest to recharge the batteries. Moreover, I want to look again at the partnership of Niall Quinn and David Kelly which did so well in Cork last month.

Quinn hasn't started a senior international game in almost two years but his form since joining Manchester City from Arsenal is the talk of England. The lad has regained his self-belief and in that mood, he is capable of troubling any defence. Kelly, too, is beginning to buzz again. He has put his name on some fine goals for Leicester City in recent weeks and is now champing at the bit for the opportunity to carry that form into international football.

By leaving out Bonner, I am able to catch up on lost time and give Gerry Peyton the chance of reacclimatising with our back four. Remember this was the game plan for Wales but, unfortunately, it had to be shelved when Gerry pulled out of the squad.

This is an ideal occasion to bring Paul McGrath back into the side after sitting out the Welsh fixture. I am anxious to see how he moves in central midfield . . . to assess how his knees are standing up to the wear and tear of the season.

It was also my intention to use Chris Hughton at some stage. The idea was to move Steve Staunton into midfield and bring in Chris at left back but it didn't quite work out like that. At the pre-arranged time for Chris to make his entrance, we had just gone ahead and I have to admit that pragmatism took over. Experimentation is one thing but on this occasion, it had to be measured against the psychological advantage of a win over the Soviets.

It is an achievement for any team to beat the Soviet Union and I decided to protect the lead rather than get too ambitious and start pulling players around. In fact, Chris got into the team for the last 15 minutes or so but not at left back. He was slotted in on the opposite flank after Chris Morris had gone off injured.

The match, as it turned out, was memorable only for the fact that we went on to make it 19 games on the trot without defeat in Dublin. The Soviets simply did not want to know about opening up the game for an hour and as a consequence, scoring opportunities were few.

To be honest, I didn't expect much more. Nobody wants to be beaten less than two months before the World Cup finals and Lobanovsky, it seemed to me, travelled to Dublin to get a scoreless draw.

Yet, it was a good experience for our players, not least in the fact that it reacquainted them with the hazards of facing a sweeper. Vaghiz Khidiatulin filled the role for the Soviets and some of the professional commentators were ecstatic about his performance. I was less impressed. A good sweeper, in my book, is not just a player who tidies up at the back but is ready and able to join in the scheme of things going forward.

Khidiatulin did none of this at Lansdowne. He just sat in and filled the hole without ever attempting to break into our half of the pitch. I think the 44,000 spectators in the stadium were entitled to expect more from a player of his stature.

The opening half of the game was pretty drab but it perked up subsequently to provide a little more goalmouth action. Ironically, it was a dreadful decision by the American referee, Alfred Kleinaitis, against Paul McGrath which stirred the fans and, ultimately, the Irish players into action. For the first time, perhaps, we began to put them under concerted pressure and that was down to the fact that McGrath and Andy Townsend were more adventurous in getting forward. It was one such break by Townsend which led to the decisive goal in the 65th minute.

It ended with Andy forcing Vladimir Tishenko to handle just outside the penalty area and the rest was perfection. Steve Staunton, almost standing over the ball, measured the chip so accurately that goalkeeper Uvarov hadn't a chance of getting to it as it dipped just beneath the angle of the upright and the crossbar.

I can stick my chest out and say that we rehearsed the move in training the previous day. What I don't like to admit is that there was an element of Murphy's Law involved. In fact, Niall Quinn, a fair striker of the ball, should have hit the shot in that instance with Staunton trying his luck with free kicks on the other side of the penalty area. But 'Stan' fancied his chances of putting it away and he was as good as his word. I only wish he had been a little more patient and saved it up for Italy.

After that, we played some good football and we were just a little unfortunate not to have scored a second time when Townsend caught one on the full, only to see Uvarov produce the save of the game. However, we had one or two bad moments in the closing minutes. It was only after they had fallen behind that the Soviets decided to come and have a go at us. And when they did, they showed that they could be quite dangerous.

The other factor in the turnabout was that we began to lose our shape a little after first Morris and then O'Leary had departed with injuries. It meant that we weren't as tight as we had been and I think that gave the Soviets a little extra confidence.

They could and perhaps should have equalised when a misplaced header by McCarthy gave Yuri Savichev a clear run at goal but with only Gerry Peyton to beat, he lost his nerve and shot wide. The buildup to that incident was interesting for it was a replica of the move which caught us cold for the Soviets' equaliser in West Germany two years earlier.

Interspersed with the normal pattern of their short game, they occasionally play the long, diagonal ball from one of the full back positions for a player running into an inside forward position. I had warned our players of this ploy and in fairness to McCarthy, he read it well. Unfortunately for him the ball swung in the air and instead of making the decisive clearance, it caught him on the back of the head and dropped into danger territory.

Predictably enough, the McCarthy-bashers seized on that incident in an attempt to prove yet again that he was vulnerable but it didn't wash with me. If anybody erred in that instance, it was O'Leary who, instead of falling in behind Mick to provide cover, was standing too square when McCarthy miscued the header.

I was more annoyed by the mistake which nearly let in Igor Belanov in the last couple of minutes. By this time, Kevin Moran had replaced O'Leary and he was pretty close to being punished when Savichev threaded the ball through to Belanov.

A defence normally only gets into trouble when it allows an opponent turn to make the final pass. We forgot this basic rule after Savichev had moved on to the ball and it very nearly cost us.

Yet, it has been a worthwhile exercise. Even without Houghton and Whelan, our midfield performed well with McGrath and Townsend particularly effective when they decided to run at the Soviets in the second half.

Inevitably, perhaps, I was more interested in the performances of those coming into the side and in each case I thought they did well. Peyton wasn't required to work overtime but one good stop early in the second half proved that his reflexes are as sharp as ever. Waddock, too, had some good moments down the right side of midfield and if neither Quinn nor Kelly got any shots on target, they competed and supported well. It is never easy trying to outwit a defence which deploys a sweeper but they stuck to the job well and will have profited from the experience.

Leaving Lansdowne Road this evening, I am more convinced than ever of the morale of the squad. Nobody, not even the Soviets, can intimidate us and looking further ahead to the 1992 European championships, it will take a hell of a good team to get a result against us in Dublin.

Yet, even as we savour our victory and the statisticians get to work analysing the implications of this latest performance, I know it will be a different ball game if we meet the Soviet Union in Italy.

THURSDAY 17
May 1990

●

From a long way back, I sensed that yesterday's game against Finland at Lansdowne Road, our last home fixture before heading off to the finals, would be unusually troublesome. Unfortunately, my worst fears were realised.

That assessment, I hasten to add, had nothing to do with the Finns. They have always been strong and athletic, and when it comes to running, they are right up there with the best of them. But Finland, as a football nation, have never been particularly clever, technically or tactically, and in the normal course of events they would not have been my choice of opposition at this late stage of our preparations for the World Cup.

The reality, of course, is that the game was staged as a testimonial for Liam Brady. He was responsible for the match arrangements, including the chore of wheeling and dealing with the agents of national associations and, to be fair to him, he tried desperately hard to get one of the better international teams before settling reluctantly for Finland.

No, the Finns as a team didn't bother me, but the designation of the match did. As I saw it, it was neither an international nor a testimonial match and my great fear was that it would fall into the gulf between the two. Unhappily, I was proved right. My other concern was that it would revive the controversy about Liam Brady himself and his decision to opt out of international football, announced last September.

I've already written about the pros and cons of that situation. But sure as hell, I knew that I would be landed right back in the middle of the debate if Liam played against Finland. Tradition demands that the beneficiary plays in his own testimonial. So for better or worse, I named Brady in the starting line-up on the understanding that he would be taken off after 20 minutes.

That decision was fraught with risk. We were, after all, dealing with a national hero, a man identified by the fans as the very essence of the game in Ireland. Anything which was seen as diminishing that status would be resented. I knew the script and I knew the consequences but I also knew my obligations to the team. So five minutes past the appointed time I got up from the dug-out and gestured to Liam to come in. Some people were incensed.

In today's papers, I read about him having a great game. That is rubbish. Liam played reasonably well, but no more than that. And the football we saw at Lansdowne last evening was light years removed from the challenges we will face in Italy. It gave me no pleasure to call the shots as I saw them. I, too, was sad at the loss of a once great player and I was genuinely delighted that the disappointment for him was cushioned by a big paynight. But some of the stuff that was written and spoken appalled me. I went along with Maurice Setters to Liam's testimonial dinner and had a great night until Ray Treacy got up to pay his tribute.

Treacy went on to berate our style of play, implying that we depended on sweat and workrate to compensate for skill and that

Liam could still redress that imbalance. What a load of poppycock! Sure, we place heavy emphasis on fitness and running power. But to imply that we are short of skill is to overlook the presence of players like Ronnie Whelan, Ray Houghton, Kevin Sheedy and Andy Townsend in midfield. This was neither the time nor the place for comments like that and I felt Treacy was out of order.

As I said earlier, some Irish people live too often in the past for their own good and all this nonsense about Brady being in some way or another victimised for the World Cup is based solely on what he has achieved in the past. Nobody would have been happier to have him in our squad than me if I felt that he could still do it for us at this level. But that, of course, is not the case.

Talking of long memories, I found it strange that in all the hype about Liam, nobody once mentioned the name of Tony Galvin. He too had been a valuable member of the squad for a number of years and was now cruelly robbed of the chance of going to Italy because of injury. The lad's loyalty and sense of commitment to the Irish team has been unquestioned and yet he hasn't rated a mention when it comes to the hard-luck stories of the World Cup. I found difficulty in reconciling that omission with the hype about Liam.

I was also intensely annoyed when I heard Gay Byrne joining the bandwagon this morning by inviting listeners to the radio programme to lobby for Liam's return. Gay is a super broadcaster and a good friend of the Irish team but he's no expert on football and never was. The matter of selecting the Irish team has nothing to do with him or his listeners or indeed the public at large. The FAI pay me to select and prepare the national team and I'll do that job without interference from anybody. The day that I have to pick the side by national referendum is the day that I am surplus to requirements and I quit.

When I compiled my original squad of 19 players for the Finnish game, I did so in the knowledge that three of them, Kevin Moran, Frank Stapleton and Alan McLoughlin would probably be involved in the Swindon Town–Blackburn Second Division play-off game on the same night. I was still hopeful that circumstances would contrive to make them available to us. But deep down I sensed the worst and structured the squad accordingly. Sure enough, all three were pulled out by their clubs a couple of days before the game.

John Aldridge was back with us for the first time since the game against Malta. But delighted as I was to have him in the squad, I decided that I would leave him on the bench and start with Bernie Slaven and Tony Cascarino up front. The reasoning behind that decision was to settle Slaven into our team pattern. Aldridge had been with us for four years, he knew exactly what we required of our front runners and barring the unforeseen, he would be in our starting line-up in Italy.

Slaven was different. He had played just once for us against Wales and while he did quite well, I needed further proof before deciding that he could contribute to our plans in Italy. I didn't have any real doubts about his goal-scoring ability, but I still needed to be assured on his preparedness to work and support.

Ronnie Whelan was out with a broken bone in his foot. But at that stage, ironically, I was more concerned about the fitness of his Liverpool clubmate Ray Houghton who had been suffering from a back injury for much of the season. Broken bones respond to treatment and in time, mend, but dodgy backs are different. You go to bed feeling OK and wake up in the morning crocked. Scenarios like that haunt players and managers alike and there were occasions when I woke up in a cold sweat worrying about Houghton.

He was, and is, indispensable to our match plan and the thought of having to take on England without him, was almost too bleak to contemplate. As it turned out, Ray had a fine game and I was able to sleep easy last night.

Mind you, there wasn't much else in the match to satisfy. It was, without a shadow of a doubt, a most unsatisfactory game from my point of view, lacking continuity and most of the qualities of a real international occasion. That was down, in part, to the fact that there were so many substitutions that it never developed an established pattern. It may also have had something to do with the presence of Liam Brady. To accommodate Liam, we had to make concessions to our normal style and even when he was withdrawn and replaced by Andy Townsend, we failed to get any real bite into our play.

Finland as ever, were strong and enthusiastic, but I think we made them look a better side than they actually are. Yet, the fact is that we came within a couple of minutes of surrendering our unbeaten record in Dublin and had it panned out like that, we could have only blamed ourselves.

Over a period of time, we have developed our game to the point where we expect players like Tony Cascarino and Mick McCarthy to win everything in the air. But last evening, it didn't work out like that. The big Finns clattered into Cascarino every time the ball was hoisted into their penalty area and even Mick, for once, found difficulty in dominating his own penalty area. Yet they never really troubled us at the back until they hit us with a beautiful goal nine minutes from the end. McCarthy's headed clearance was caught on the volley just outside the penalty area and it sailed over Paddy Bonner's head into the net. The ball, I felt, could have gone anywhere, but this was the one-in-ten shot and the Finn may have been as surprised as anybody when he saw it dip in beneath the crossbar for as good a goal as you will see anywhere.

We don't concede too many scores in Dublin and when it happens the inquests tend to be long and hard. But on this occasion, the consensus was that it was a freak and nobody was to blame.

McCarthy, under pressure, wasn't to know the consequences of his clearance and Bonner, a couple of yards off his line, had taken up the position that I would expect of him. So it was a case of all credit to the Finn and no blame to any of our people.

The effect was to galvanise the Irish team into action and for the next nine minutes we lifted our game in a manner which contrasted with much of what had gone before. By lifting the tempo, we immediately put the visitors under

The Russian goalkeeper
arov outjumps Niall Quinn

△
◁ Bernie Slaven in action
against the Welsh.

△
The win against Wales
maintained our great record
at Lansdowne Road.

David Kelly challenges
Tischenko in the Russian
match at Lansdowne Road. ▷

△ It wasn't all hard work in Turkey. Here, Maurice Setters walks past a relaxed Irish squad!

△ Long before a ball was kicked in Italy, the press conference was a daily ritual.

Squad training is as much about planning and talking as about playing.

△ Just to prove I can still do it!

The contrast between the English and Irish fans is summed up in these pictures. Everywhere they went, the English were a security problem. Our lads had fun, caused no trouble and even got in the odd game themselves.

Lineker's early goal in the England game was a real sickener.

△ Paul McGrath and John Barnes.

△ His left foot! Kevin Sheedy's equaliser against England.

△ Bryan Robson is challenged by Chris Morris.

Two shots of John Aldridge in action against the Egyptians.

△ Kevin Sheedy got in this spectacular volley against Egypt.

Tony Cascarino's strength in the air troubled the Egyptians, even if occasionally he needed a hand from his mates!

Ruud Gullit in action against us. This fine sportsman showed something like his true form in Palermo.

pressure and before the Finns quite realised what was happening, we were level again.

I had taken Slaven out of the game sometime earlier to give Aldridge a run and it was John who set up the equaliser after Houghton had provided the cross from the right. Aldo was a bit unfortunate to see the goalkeeper push his shot on to the crossbar but before the defence could recover, Kevin Sheedy was in to put the rebound in the net.

At that point we were really motoring but sadly time ran out on us and we had to settle in the end for a 1–1 draw. The only consolation on a disappointing day was that it could have been so much worse.

The Finnish game was not of course the only one which concerned us this week. On Tuesday night our 'B' team was in action against Northern Ireland in Portadown and while a 3–2 win was not, on the face of it, a world-shattering performance our team showed a lot of character in coming back from a two-goal deficit. I was particularly interested in the reports on Niall Quinn and David Kelly, who had done the business for us so successfully in Cork and who were now teaming up again in the centre of the attack. Maurice Setters, who took charge of the team that night, was happy with the form of both players and it was good to see David on target again with two goals. It confirmed that the lad's confidence was flowing again and that was an encouraging sign in the run-up to the finals.

But neither that result nor indeed the one at Lansdowne registered with the public quite as much as the scoreline from Aberdeen

where Egypt, against all the odds, got a shock 3–1 win over Scotland. Results in the months and weeks before a major event like the World Cup or European championship are notoriously unreliable and as such ought not receive too much attention. Yet, the very idea of a team like Egypt going to Aberdeen and achieving a win of those proportions was jarring.

The Egyptians, for many, were the fall guys in our group, the team which would provide the other three with an easy win. I certainly don't regard them as such but I have to say that I was amazed when I watched highlights of the match on television.

In a sense it wasn't a case of what Egypt did as what Scotland didn't do, but that wasn't the whole story either. I was staggered by some of the mistakes the Scots made and yet there was a lot to recommend Egypt's performance. I watched them in Cairo earlier in the year and was reported in the press as saying that I wasn't impressed. In fact, I said nothing of the kind. I thought they had some good technical players, were tactically alert and when the opportunity arose were quite sharp on the break. That last point was perfectly illustrated in their third goal at Hampden.

After shooting themselves in both feet the Scots clawed their way back into the game at 2–1 and were committing a lot of players in the search for the equaliser. Teams are always vulnerable in that situation and the Egyptians punished them mercilessly on the counter-attack. That was a painful experience for Scotland, but a very useful lesson for us. It put us on our guard for Sicily and that was beneficial for our players and supporters alike.

Egypt will be no easy touch for anybody. My trip to Cairo convinced me of that but I still reckon that they will have more problems in coping with our brand of football than they will have against England or Holland.

England were also in action this week, beating Denmark 1–0 at Wembley. It gave them their 18th win on the trot and the scoreline was almost certainly the most rewarding part of the evening for Bobby Robson. I didn't think they played particularly well, being caught offside too often against a team which was well organised and succeeded in defying all effort to break them down until Gary Lineker pounced for one of his special scores.

The most interesting part of the game for me was a subtle change in tactics by the English. When we played them in Stuttgart two years earlier, their main strategy was the long ball played in behind our central defenders by Glen Hoddle. At the time, Hoddle was one of the best players in the world in that aspect of the game and he got us into trouble too often for the good of our health.

In fact, Paddy Bonner was responsible for aggravating the problem. Bonner pulled off some super saves that day and some people thought that I had lost my reason when I had a go at him after the game. I still believe I was right. Had he come off his line as he was told he would have snuffed out the threat before people like Lineker and Beardsley got near the ball.

But now, two years on, England's strategy was different. The front runners were dropping off and laying the ball off for people like Bryan Robson and Steve Hodge steaming through the middle. It's a ploy which is used a lot on the Continent but in the Denmark game, at least, England's timing was not sufficiently precise to prevent people running offside.

Yet our defenders have been warned as to what they can expect in Cagliari. How they react to the challenge will determine to a large extent how that game will go. Inevitably, it will put our central defenders under the spotlight and just as surely prompt the knockers to have another go at Mick McCarthy and Kevin Moran and their alleged lack of pace. I have been listening to that kind of criticism for the better part of four years and smiling to myself. They were saying much the same thing about Alan Hansen and other people in the Liverpool defence four years ago and you know how wrong they were in that instance.

FRIDAY 18
May 1990

●

The hype is growing to such an extent that I am delighted to be able to escape for four days' fishing in Co. Galway before setting off for Italy.

World Cup fever is one thing and I am happy to share in the fans' sense of expectancy. But darn it, there are more things to life than football.

Because of my public-speaking engagements I have had to cut back on my shooting and fishing. And believe you me, that hurts. Ever since I quit club football I have set aside two days a week when I could take myself out into the country and have a good time. Unfortunately, that little treat went out the window as my diary began to fill with more and more engagements. But when I got the opportunity to go fishing in Galway with a couple of old pals, I decided that nothing, bar nothing, would prevent me accepting it.

The players, too, are beginning to feel the pinch but for them, the ordeal is one of tiredness rather than pressure. When you play for clubs like Liverpool and Arsenal, every game is important and you soon learn to live with pressure. Physical weariness is different. All the lads have been involved with their clubs since last August and now, almost ten months later, they are being asked to lift themselves again and get ready for the biggest challenge of their careers.

Some of those involved in the Second Division promotion play-offs, will still be playing club football next week. That is not the ideal preparation for an event like the World Cup. It brings to mind again the folly of English clubs having to play sixty games or more in a season and the undue demands the system places on international footballers. That is why I don't regard Ronnie Whelan's foot injury as the tragedy which some of the critics would have us believe. It is, of course, worrying but the good thing about it is that it gives him a respite from competition.

He has been playing twice a week for Liverpool since the start of the season and more than most, he needs a rest to recharge the batteries.

With the Finland game out of the way, I have sent the lads home for a week's holiday and the chance to tidy up family affairs. They will be away from home for four or five weeks and they need time to themselves to get things in order.

As for me, Galway here I come.

FRIDAY 25
May 1990

●

It was ironic that when we assembled at Dublin Airport at 7 a.m. this morning, at the start of the journey to Izmir, the one name which dominated the conversation was Bobby Robson.

Ever since we discovered that we had to open our programme against England, Robson has lain heavily on our minds. But our concern now has less to do with football matters than the disclosure only yesterday that he is quitting as England's manager after the World Cup to talk to the Dutch club, PSV Eindhoven.

Fair enough, that is his prerogative. But what is not acceptable is the manner in which the tabloid press have handled the story. To start, they miscalculated and reckoned that Bobby's letter of impending resignation had to do with his private life. Perhaps it suited their purpose to do so, for it gave them the chance of digging up, yet again, an affair which he was supposed to have had years ago. Now, when it is clear that this is not the case, they are laying into him as only they can. For years they have been looking for his scalp, often inventing reasons why he should be sacked. Now he is going to oblige them by leaving and what do they do? They call him a traitor. There is nothing too low for them.

I looked around the plane this morning and noted the reaction of the players to the story. There was nobody laughing, nobody taking the mickey, for they, like me, were appalled by the way that the hatchet job had been performed.

Bobby's predicament has some relevance for them. Here they are about to embark on the biggest adventure of their careers and their every move will be noted by the press people travelling with us. Last evening I took them aside and told them precisely what was what. Footballers are normal, healthy young men who can get up to precisely the same things as any people of their age group. Normally, it's just innocent fun but just occasionally somebody breaks the rules and when that happens I sort out the situation fast and we're able to get back to basics again.

But World Cup and European championship finals are different. Almost by definition, they attract high profiles in the media and that puts the players under the microscope all the time. The regular journalists on the international scene are no problem. They know us and we know them and the relationship is generally one of trust. The journalists who worry us are the fringe people, the news reporters who normally have little to do with football. In many cases, these people are looking for scandal, not necessarily major stuff but small, isolated incidents which can be blown up out of all proportion. I am determined that they will not be given that opportunity in Italy.

The send-off for the squad in Dublin was well intentioned but at that hour of the morning, I thought it was a little bit over the top. Arnold O'Byrne of Opel had even organised a band from Sardinia to play us out on to the tarmac and there seemed to be television cameras everywhere.

I appreciated the sentiments but I'm afraid I'm not at my perkiest at that hour of the morning. I was glad when we were eventually airborne and we could reapply our minds to the main business of the day.

I want this game in Turkey on the way to our pre-World Cup base in Malta, primarily to familiarise the squad with the type of conditions they can expect in Italy. I was not to know at the time that the draw for the qualifying rounds of the 1992 European championship in Sweden, would lump us with the Turks.

With this friendly game thrown in, it means that we will be playing them three times in the space of 18 months. But just now, I am more concerned that they can get us in the right shape for the World Cup.

Turkey have always been a reasonably good technical team who could knock it about a bit and unless I am greatly mistaken, they will stretch us in the sun. A year ago they beat Austria 3–0 at home, a result which has been put in good perspective by the Austrians' subsequent performances.

Additionally, they have now acquired the services of Sepp Piontek, the shrewd West German who, in his time, built Denmark into one of the most attractive teams in the world. Sepp has now embarked on the task of revitalising Turkey's fortunes. As luck would have it, one of the first people I met when we checked into our hotel in Izmir was Sepp, returning from a training session with his team. The look on their faces told all.

It was hot outside and if the Turks who were familiar with these conditions were sweating up so much, heaven knows what effects the burning sun would have on our lot.

We didn't have to wait long to find out. We went to the match stadium within a couple of hours of our arrival and discovered that the heat in the bowl-shaped arena was, indeed, something else. Given the fact that Sunday's game will be played in mid-afternoon, it is apparent that our players are going to earn their money the hard way.

Heat or no heat, however, I decided to train the effects of the long air trip out of their systems immediately. Most of them had done no serious training for a fortnight and it was essential that we make a start right away.

The first setback of the trip wasn't long delayed. While the rest of the players with the exception of Ronnie Whelan and Kevin Moran got stuck in immediately, I noticed that Ray Houghton was taking no part. Ray had a variety of problems throughout the season, ranging from back trouble to a damaged hamstring, but my information was that he was now in the clear. As it happened, I had a few shocks coming.

I asked him what the problem was and I nearly dropped on the spot when he told me he had a pelvic strain. This is one of the most serious injuries in football and here I was listening to one of my key players telling me that he had, somehow, drawn the booby prize. My initial reaction was one of annoyance as much as disappointment. I felt he should have acquainted me of the situation earlier and if he really had a pelvic injury, he would be better off at home.

I have decided to take some medical advice on the problem tomorrow. But this is not the kind of start that is calculated to inspire confidence. Apart from Houghton, Whelan struggled having had the plaster removed from a foot injury only three days ago and Moran, of course, was recovering from a damaged Achilles tendon sustained in Blackburn's play-off against Swindon.

The mood, I can assure you, was sombre when we got back to the hotel after training. But damn it, it's only a game and when the initial shock had subsided, Maurice Setters and I went out for a few drinks with some press people and I even sang a few verses of The Bladon Races. Tomorrow is another day.

SATURDAY 26
May 1990
●

Mick Byrne, our physiotherapist, is one of the most valuable members of our technical staff. He knows his job intimately, enjoys the confidence of the players and at times is as much a psychologist to the team as a physiotherapist. So it was encouraging that, when we trained this morning, he

△ Here we go! The scene at Dublin Airport as we left for the great adventure.

△ Press conferences were a regular feature of the whole trip right from the start. With one or two exceptions, the press were good to us and I think we were good to them.

It was incredibly hot in Izmir for the Turkish match but the whole team stuck to its task with great spirit. I reckoned that this game would get the lads acclimatised to playing in really hot conditions. In fact, it turned out to be the hottest day of the whole trip.

Kevin Moran in action against Malta.

lost no time in telling me that, in his opinion, all three injured players would be fit for the England game.

That is fine but, at the end of the day, only the players can tell me how they have recovered. They might be influenced by what Mick told them but, deep down, each and every one of them would have to make that decision for himself.

Footballers as a breed are basically honest people and I now have to put my trust in their integrity. As professionals, they are preparing to play on the biggest stage of all and it is essential that they level with themselves and with me.

I told Kevin, Ray and Ronnie to go away and think about it and to let me know precisely what they thought of their chances of recovering. If they are going to stay with us, it is essential they be fit enough to contribute to the team.

Later, we had Houghton x-rayed and medical opinion was that if he worked on the injury, with particular emphasis on stretching, he would be ready for the England game. It was pointed out to me that his was the kind of strain that would come and go from one day to another but he is such a vital cog in the machine that I felt obliged to take the chance.

Ronnie Whelan had shed a lot of muscle in his injured leg during his lay-off but with hard work, he can put it back on over the next ten days. The bigger worry by far is the fact that he hasn't played a game for five weeks and I suspect that this could affect his movement and rhythm.

Kevin Moran came to me and said he was pretty certain that he would be fit for Cagliari. He also asked me if I had made up my mind about my back four for the World Cup, and I told him in all honesty that I hadn't.

A couple of months ago, it was different, Moran had been one of the anchor men of the side and, fitness permitting, I would always have him in at centre back. But now the situation has changed.

David O'Leary has come into the team and done well in every game and has implanted a doubt in my mind. And I hasten to add that it is not the kind of doubt I ever entertained when half of Ireland was campaigning for his inclusion in the squad for the European championships.

I didn't select him then because I believed that I had two better central defenders in McCarthy and Moran and no amount of public lobbying would or could change that. But as I see it, we are now into a different ball game.

O'Leary has again proved himself as a top-class international player over a period of 18 months. His partnership with McCarthy looks sound to me and I now have a difficult choice to make in choosing two from three.

In any event, I don't have any option but to go with McCarthy and O'Leary for the Turkish game. I also think that the time is opportune to bring back John Aldridge to partner Tony Cascarino in the front line.

Cass looked a little bit heavy and ponderous in his movement when we trained and I reckon that he needs a hard game to get back into shape. Given the weather conditions, he will get all of that tomorrow.

With Houghton and Whelan out, Paul McGrath and Andy Townsend are automatic choices in central midfield and Gary Waddock will fill in on the right side of midfield.

Waddock is, for some, a surprising choice in the squad for Turkey. But I think he did quite well in the game against the Soviet Union and in view of all that he has been through, I reckon he deserves the chance to show what he can do.

On the other flank in midfield, Kevin Sheedy also needs a hard game at this point. Sheedy is not the most aggressive of runners but in the new priorities which the heat and humidity impose, he will have a vital role to play.

At the team talk this evening, I laid our strategy on the line. We haven't lost a game abroad since the defeat by Spain in Seville eighteen months ago. That is a record that I don't want to put at undue risk; and yet the scoreline will not be the most important aspect of the game. The primary aim is to familiarise ourselves with the match conditions we can expect in Italy.

We will have to learn how and when to take a rest in the game without disclosing our hand to the opposition. Instead of going and running for 90 minutes, we will sit tight for periods, upping the tempo of our game only occasionally.

The slow-slow, quick-quick game, favoured by so many European teams, doesn't come easily to the home countries. But no less than the heat, we will have to come to terms with that particular challenge if we are to leave our imprint on the championship.

SUNDAY 27
May 1990

●

This morning proved one thing beyond question. If we need to be subjected to unusual conditions to test our powers of recovery, we have certainly come to the right place.

A hot sun shone out of the sky over Izmir and by the time we got to the Ataturk Stadium, it was so warm that the slightest movement meant a loss of sweat. That was good. Sweating cools the body and before we set down in Italy, we would have to sweat and sweat again to be able to compete on equitable terms.

We learned later that the temperature this afternoon was 106 degrees, the warmest May day Izmir has known in fifty years and one that had even the locals gasping for breath.

In those circumstances, it was scarcely surprising that we didn't win the game. But then we didn't lose it either. A scoreless draw was always on the cards and as the match panned out, it became more and more inevitable that the first goal would win it.

For the 200 or so Irish supporters sandwiched into a noisy crowd of 40,000, our type of game must have looked strange in the extreme. For example, we were playing the ball around at the back, knocking it square and occasionally slowing the game to a crawl.

Those kind of tactics are foreign to my usual thinking on football and how you play it. But when in Turkey, do as the Turks do.

That is not to say that I was wholly satisfied with our performance. I wasn't. One or two of our players seemed to be too apprehensive about the heat and a couple more looked in need of the game. I felt there were times when we lacked conviction in closing down people and we did not give Aldridge the support he needed when he got on the ball. And that was an important lesson which needed to be absorbed.

Our policy was to contain energy and push forward only when we considered it was appropriate. But once we decide to go, we've got to do so as if we really mean it. Because of the conditions, we didn't do that often enough today and it showed.

In a sense, it derived from the fact that we had to play with a rebuilt midfield formation. The first and most fundamental part of closing down a team is to push on to players and not give them a line of escape.

We didn't do that against the Turks and the result was that they were able to play their way out of trouble in situations where it ought to have been impossible. Against a team of the quality of Holland or England, that could have been disastrous.

Technically, Turkey are not a bad side as they showed late in the game when a mistake by Chris Morris gave them their only real chance of the afternoon. But we survived that crisis and from then on, it was plain sailing for our defence.

We didn't create too many scoring opportunities ourselves and that could be written off in part to two over-zealous linesmen. Every time Cascarino and Aldridge got the ball in any kind of dangerous position, they were flagged. I dread the thought that it could set the pattern for Italy.

The Soviet referee, Alexander Kirkov, was no great shakes either and I thought that he was wrong in whistling back Bernie Slaven after he had put the ball in the net six minutes from the end. Initially, he didn't appear to have any doubt that John Byrne had won the ball fairly in a tackle with Kemal near the back line and it wasn't until the cross was already launched, that he blew for a foul by Byrne.

Slaven certainly wasn't aware of the whistle when he met the cross perfectly with his head to pick his spot in the net and that impressed me. The lad is growing up fast in the special demands of international football.

On the credit side of things, I thought Paul McGrath had another superb game in midfield and when he dropped back into the defence after David O'Leary had gone off, he showed so much composure on the ball that at times it looked unreal. As I saw it, he was miles ahead of anybody else on the park.

I thought there was also a lot to admire about the way McCarthy and O'Leary handled things in central defence and there was only one word to describe the efforts of Cascarino and Aldridge—brave.

Theirs were always going to be the most difficult roles of all for while others could take the occasional rest and get away with it, they were required to work all the time. And to their credit, they never shirked the job.

A week ago, there had been a hue and cry about the players' bonuses. Some people felt they were getting too much, others not enough. But those in the first category should have felt the shirts Cascarino and Aldridge were wearing today. They were simply saturated with sweat.

I could have taken either or both players off and sent on Niall Quinn and David Kelly to give us an extra bit of pace and movement. But that would have defeated the purpose of the game. I needed to know how both players would react under highly stressed conditions in the sun and I had got the answer. Neither man would short-change the team in the World Cup finals.

Waddock, I'm afraid, didn't quite do the job I had asked of him. But John Byrne looked the part when he replaced him and John Sheridan, another of the four substitutes used, was a lot more fluent than in the match with Wales.

The downside of the operation was that neither of our full backs, Chris Morris and Steve Staunton, impressed. Staunton was so laid back that it wasn't funny and I doubt if he made one tackle of note before he was replaced by Chris Hughton early in the second half.

Chris, I thought, did an infinitely better job, getting in fast and tight on his man in addition to providing the necessary support down the left. For him, it has been a rewarding day.

It took our lads longer than usual to get changed afterwards and that was the consequence of 90 minutes work under a cruel sun. Some like Chris Hughton said that the heat hadn't bothered them but for the rest, it was all pretty punishing.

Moreover David O'Leary and Andy Townsend picked up injuries and given the other casualties in the squad, that is an added complication which we can do without.

MONDAY 28
May 1990

●

Today we made a tough journey from Izmir to our pre-World Cup base in Malta. It took us through Istanbul and Rome and ended some ten hours after it began at Rabat just outside Valetta.

We are now just 24 hours away from the deadline for naming the 22 players for the finals to FIFA officials in Rome.

It should be a relatively straightforward task for when you boil it all down, we don't have many more than 22 players of international calibre. However, that is precisely why I now find myself in such a quandary.

I have three fairly serious casualties in the squad, Ray Houghton, Ronnie Whelan and Kevin Moran, and two more—David O'Leary and Andy Townsend—of whom I can't be 100% certain.

Houghton's injury is particularly serious because it can vary from day to day. That is a manager's nightmare for it means that you cannot make any kind of plan, even in the short term.

The logical solution would be to send the player home, and I might have done so days ago if I had a replacement of reasonable standard available to me. But that, of course, is not the case. We are not

Italy or Brazil. I'll have to take a chance. I'll include Whelan, Houghton and Moran in the list and hope and pray that time will prove me right.

The risk is that I could go to Cagliari with only 19 fit players and with the probability of further mishaps along the way. But just now, it looks to me the lesser of two evils.

But this solution creates another problem. While I am prepared to sit and wait for Whelan and Houghton to recover, I have to have some kind of contingency plan in place.

There is nobody here capable of doing Houghton's job and if the worst comes to the worst I am going to end up with a wholly unbalanced line across the middle. So I am going to call up Alan McLoughlin of Swindon Town. I know I said that I would never bring an uncapped player to Italy and in the normal course of events I wouldn't take the chance.

But necessity is the mother of invention. In fact it isn't even all that big of a risk, for the lad would have been in the team had Swindon's commitments not prevented him from travelling to Dublin for our end of season games against the Soviet Union and Finland. Both Maurice and I had been enormously impressed when we watched him in action for Swindon—even more so by the manner in which he settled in to run midfield in the 'B' international against England.

He is a strong, skilful carrier of the ball whose role at Swindon demands that he runs at defenders. For all his immaturity, I am prepared to gamble that he can do a useful job for us if Whelan and Houghton both lost out in their race against time.

The dilemma now was who to leave out to accommodate McLoughlin. Eventually I decided that Gary Waddock would have to go—and that nearly broke my heart.

There is no braver player around than Gary for the simple reason that nobody has had to show as much bravery as he. It was courage as much as skill which got him back into the game after he had been written off by QPR and when I told him that he was coming to Turkey with us, he must have felt that all his birthdays had arrived together. Yet here I was, less than a fortnight later, obliged to inform him that it was a false start and that he would not, after all, be a member of the World Cup squad. It was one of my most difficult moments as Irish manager.

I told him when we were waiting at the airport. When you have bad news like that to impart, there is no such thing as an ideal place to deliver the word. I was sincere when I said that my decision did not necessarily mean that he was inferior to McLoughlin as a player. Their styles were different and it just happened that we needed Alan with us to give us more balance.

To his credit, Gary put a brave face on what must have been a crushing disappointment. He wished both Alan and the team the best of luck but decided that he didn't want to remain on with the party as an official guest of the FAI. He told me that he would take the first available flight back to London and I suppose I couldn't blame him. He had just seen his hopes of playing in the World Cup finals blown apart. Perhaps his big chance will come again.

This evening Maurice and I have gone through the formality of compiling the list which will be transmitted to FIFA in the morning. The final stage of our World Cup preparations is under way!

TUESDAY 29
May 1990

●

It is, I think, fair to say that 90 per cent of the people who take a genuine interest in the Republic of Ireland team could have predicted, with a fair degree of certainty, the names of at least 20 of the 22 players I am taking to Italy.

We don't have the depth in numbers that other countries possess but, that is not necessarily a bad thing. Smallness is the father of togetherness and it accounts for the fact that ours is probably the happiest, most tightly knit squad to be found anywhere in the broad world of international football.

The two goalkeepers are Paddy Bonner and Gerry Peyton. Bonner, I would say without hesitation, is one of the best 'keepers in Europe, a point he proved with some spectacular performances in the European finals in West Germany and again in the World Cup qualifying series.

With any successful team, you hope that your outfield players are sufficiently well organised to deny the opposition many clear sightings of goal. But when the outer ring is breached, you pray that your 'keeper will be able to cope.

Above all else, then, concentration and the ability to read the game from first minute to last, is the essence of modern goalkeeping and I feel Pakie has mastered the challenge well. With the two centre backs pushing up on to the players in front of them, our type of game demands that the goalkeeper acts as a sweeper and in that role, he has been a big success.

There was a time when English people didn't have a particularly high opinion of Scottish-based 'keepers for the very good reason that the only occasions they saw them on television they were conceding goals. And 'keepers the world over are not a pretty sight squatting on their backsides. Pakie, more than most, has given the lie to that Scottish myth and, by his attention to detail, rendered both Celtic and the Republic of Ireland magnificent service over the years.

In a specialist position such as goalkeeper adequate cover is all important and I've been happy to delegate this responsibility to Gerry Peyton since I took control of the team. In that time, Gerry has played only a handful of games but it is a tribute to the man's professionalism that his sense of dedication remains as steadfast as ever. Unlike Bonner, he hasn't enjoyed a high profile in club football but he is utterly reliable as he proved when he came in for a tricky assignment against Northern Ireland in Belfast.

One of the basic challenges in picking a squad is to balance things out in such a way that you'll be covered for any emergency. It helps to have a couple of utility players around, people who can slot into two or more positions in the event of an emergency. Against that background, I have decided to go to Italy with three full backs, Chris Morris, Steve Staunton and

Chris Hughton and two more, Paul McGrath and Ronnie Whelan, who have the happy knack of being able to do a job there.

After the European championship in 1988 I had more enquiries from journalists and European coaches about Chris Morris than any other member of our squad. I found that interesting for a number of reasons, not least for the fact that he didn't always get rave notices from the Irish press. The Continental attention, I reckon, was down to the fact that he epitomises the modern attacking full back.

Long gone are the days of the thick-thighed, thick-skulled full back whose sole responsibility was to put the opposing winger out of the game—by whatever means it took. Now they are play makers, guys who get down the line and make things happen. Morris does that job well. He's quick and incisive going forward, gets a fair proportion of his crosses on target and is now a much better player than when he first joined Celtic. I've had my differences with him about his defence but he has handled some good 'uns in his time, forwards like John Barnes, Chris Waddle and even Ruud Gullit. That kind of form will do for me.

They call Steve Staunton 'Stan' in the camp and fans sitting or standing behind the Irish bench at Lansdowne Road can vouch for the fact that I've been known to yell the name in anger. Like Morris, he tends to stand off players too often. And that is dangerous. He appears to doubt his own pace and instead of getting up tight on his winger is inclined to give him too

much time and space to get moving. Thankfully, it hasn't happened yet but one day it could prove expensive. If Stan worries about his pace, I worry sometimes about his lackadaisical attitude when he's on the ball. There is such a thing as composure but really . . .

That said, I admire him a lot. He is one of the best left-footed kickers of a ball in Europe, a big, strong lad who is going to be part of the Irish scene for a long time to come. It takes a lot of skill, commitment and occasionally luck to get into the Liverpool team, but once you have made it you mature quickly. Surrounded by good players, Staunton has made the point well over the last two seasons.

Chris Hughton is not likely to recall the 1989-90 season as one of his best. He picked up an injury early on in a pre-season game against Glasgow Rangers and while he was not to know it at the time, it turned his season at Tottenham into something of a shambles. Like the good professional that he is, however, he put his head down and battled and once he had proved his fitness, his place in the travelling party was never in any real doubt. Chris can play on either flank and, as I said, adaptability is important for it enables a manager to juggle about without interfering unduly with the basic structure of his team. More that that, however, he is a sound technical player whose pace in recovery will always give wingers problems. That facet of his game has been affected only slightly by the years and as a good supporter of the player on the ball, he is also capable of earning his keep going forward.

I am a worrier, and I don't always enjoy myself at training sessions. This was one of the exceptions.

Welcome to Cagliari! Three different views of Irish fans in the Sardinian capital.

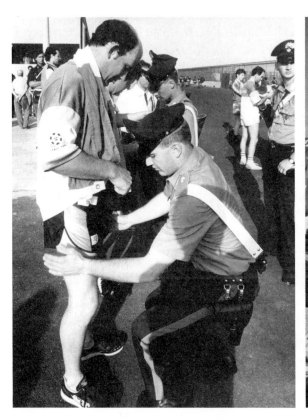

Thinking through our centre back situation has caused me more headaches in recent weeks and months than anybody will ever know. And that is surprising when you recall that I was once spoiled for choice there.

Nobody in Ireland should ever forget the contributions which Kevin Moran and Mick McCarthy have made to the evolution of our team. But as we progressed injuries eroded at least some of the magic of those marvellous moments in West Germany and again in the World Cup qualifying games.

The attitude of certain sections of the press in Ireland to McCarthy never ceases to amaze me. Nobody has given more in sweat and commitment to our cause than Mick and nobody has been more effective. Yet they continue to knock him. What do they want—blood? He's given that, too, but I'll tell you this. There are a lot of strikers around Europe who will vouch for the fact that when the challenges go in from Mick, they generally count.

The move to France was a good one for him inasmuch as it familiarised him with a different style of football but in all honesty his fitness worries me. His knees have been giving trouble for some time and they are not going to get any stronger with the years.

Kevin Moran, too, has been in the wars with injuries. For many, the move from Spanish First Division football to Blackburn Rovers wasn't progressive but I could well understand the reasons for it. In a situation in which he wasn't getting his game with FC Gijon, he felt he had to protect his World Cup place and I backed him all the way when he decided it was time to return to England.

Moran, at his best, is the perfect professional. His critics dismiss him as no more than brave and strong—and even in today's world, these are still precious qualities on a football field. That, however, is only half the story. He reads the game well, never forgets the team pattern and is a lot pacier than many think. But like McCarthy, I would like to have seen him enjoy a more settled season at club level.

While both these players were experiencing fitness problems, David O'Leary settled in early for Arsenal and we reaped the benefit in the closing stages of our qualifying programme. Having missed our European championship programme, David needed more schooling than the other players in the squad but apart from odd moments when he lapses into the role he fills at Highbury, he has proved a sharp pupil. He moves more quickly than most centre backs and once he makes contact with the player in front of him, he is firm and decisive in the tackle.

Midfield is the engine room of any team. As such, it needs a fine balance of attack and defence, strength and skill and, not least, an element of flexibility. We're lucky in so far as we have enjoyed a fairly settled midfield formation over the last couple of years and an ever present in competitive games was Ray Houghton of Liverpool.

Ray is the kind of bloke that every player likes to have in front of him. He'll work and he'll support and he'll never, ever, go missing when the action starts hotting up. That is a huge credit mark for any player and Houghton has proved in football stadia across Europe that nobody puts in more over 90 minutes.

I think his control on the ball is brilliant. He passes well, can cross with the skill of any orthodox winger and has shown himself as a decisive finisher. Remember that superb goal against Northern Ireland in Dublin! The opposition are likely to remember Houghton for the fact that he never allows them to settle on the ball, another big plus for the man whom I consider to be the best right-sided midfield player in Britain.

There were those who reckoned that when Paul McGrath left Manchester United for Aston Villa at the start of the season, his career was irreversibly in decline. Manchester United, for all their problems, are a very special club and I can well understand that when you walk out through the gates at Old Trafford for the last time, you leave something of yourself behind.

In Paul's case, however, I felt that it was a sensible move and I said so at the time. He had reached a stage in his career when he needed a change of scenery and new players around him. Graham Taylor was the kind of manager who, I thought, could coax the best out of McGrath and I was proved right.

Graham plays him mostly at centre back but I'm of the opinion that Paul's talent is wasted there. Some people are cut out to play in the position but few of them have McGrath's all-round skills of ground control, aerial power and strength in the tackle. Mark Lawrenson was a player in the same mould and I count myself fortunate that when his career was so

tragically chopped, I was able to slot McGrath into his place with the minimum period of adjustment.

I reckon one of the better things which has happened for us since the European championships has been the emergence of Andy Townsend. I was taken by his skill and his strong, direct running when I first looked at him at Norwich.

Turning on the style for Norwich is one thing but there are some, perhaps, who doubt his capacity to do a similar job for Ireland. The mark of the man is that he has taken all the qualities he has shown at Carrow Road into international football without losing anything in the transition. The point was illustrated quite brilliantly in the friendly fixture against West Germany when he came on as a replacement for Liam Brady and within minutes had changed the pattern of a game which earlier looked like running away from us. At 26, Andy is still only coming to his best and that must be a comfort to all Irish fans. He packs quite a shot, too, and when you put it all together, you get the ideal complement for Ronnie Whelan in a partnership which many managers may envy.

Kenny Dalglish, I imagine, sets about choosing his team in the same manner as I do by putting down Whelan's name first and building a side around him. That is the best tribute that you can pay a player.

Ronnie is not the kind of fellow who catches the attention of the casual onlooker. He doesn't have blonde hair, doesn't wear a sweatband and stands closer to 5ft 6ins than 6 ft. But to people in the trade, there's no one better. Somebody once said that he does the simple things better than anybody else and that is true. But when the occasion demands it, he can use the ball brilliantly as he's shown so often for Liverpool and Ireland. Ronnie is now probably at the peak of his career and I, for one, was surprised when he didn't get the player of the year award in the 1989-90 season.

With the possible exception of Chris Waddle, I would rate Kevin Sheedy as the best left-footed striker of a ball in Britain. He hits it accurately and he hits it powerfully and you cannot get much better than that. It has to be said that he is not the most aggressive of runners. But he'll pass and support and in deadball situations, he gives you some useful options. With more and more emphasis being placed on free-kick and corner-kick stategies, that is an important asset. Kevin, it is fair to say, prefers to play in central midfield but in our match plan, we use him on the flank. His is the kind of elegance that will never be out of place in international football.

Compared to many of the other big names in Britain, John Sheridan is still only an apprentice. And yet few players evoke the same sense of excitement on the terraces when he gets on to the ball in midfield. Sheridan can winkle out exquisite passes from five to fifty yards and the crowds love it. And yet he still has so much to learn. For example, he still doesn't know how to shadow a player and avoid selling himself in the tackle. Those things irritate me but he now has a good tutor at Sheffield Wednesday in the person of Ron Atkinson. In time, I think he will emerge as a great player for Ireland.

I said at the start that most of our supporters could have predicted the make-up of our squad with some confidence but few of them could have thought of Alan McLoughlin back at the start of the season.

To be honest, the name didn't mean much to me either until Tony Galvin recommended that I should take a look at him. I liked what I saw—the more so when he began to hit the target regularly from midfield for Swindon. Normally, I would back off a player who hadn't been properly versed in our system but Alan has so much going for him that I am throwing all the reservations out the door and taking him. I admire his approach to the game. He settles on the ball easily, goes at players and, most precious of all, he has the instincts of a specialist striker.

From an early stage in the qualifying series, I made up my mind that Tony Cascarino and John Aldridge were the strikers who would see us through to the finals. And this, of course, meant that Frank Stapleton had to settle for a seat on the substitutes' bench.

There are occasions when even the most hard-headed managers feel the wrench when one of their senior players comes to the end of his tether. I knew that feeling when I had to drop Frank for the first time. He was well into his career when I came to Dublin but enough of the old skill and enthusiasm survived to make him a key man in the team. Frank was a superb skipper who led from the front in Germany where only those in the know will ever appreciate the amount of work he put in.

By dropping off and plugging the gap in midfield when the opposition had the ball, he was indispensable to the system but, sadly, we knew even then that he was living on borrowed time. He can still do a useful job for us in an emergency but I'm afraid that we've seen the best of Frank.

I tried to slot Cascarino into the same role but not with any great success. He just doesn't seem to be able to get the drift of it although in every other respect, his game has developed at a remarkable rate over the last two years. He is a superb competitor who will cause problems for any centre back and his style suits our match plan perfectly. As a target man, he will never shun the responsibility of making himself available and depending on the accuracy of Paddy Bonner's clearances, that gives us a substantial advantage. Millwall's problems meant that he didn't have a great season at club level and then there was the pressure of the £1.5m move to Aston Villa. But the sight of a green shirt will always bring out the best in him and you can take it as read that nobody will push him about in the big time.

John Aldridge believes that the move from Liverpool to Spain has helped his game— and I agree with him. To those who regard Liverpool, rightly, as one of the great powers of club fooball, that may sound like heresy but it is none the less true.

Only those who have filled the role can realise how difficult life is for a striker on the Continent. At Real Sociedad, as at so many other clubs, they tend to isolate the front man. In the course of 90 minutes, he may get no more than two touches of the ball in and around the penalty area. And

he is expected to make them count. That teaches the value of concentration and as a result, Aldo was better prepared for Italy than if he had stayed at Anfield. Moreover, he has rounded his game without sacrificing any of the running power on which we depend so much. There were people who questioned our faith in John at a time when he was struggling to adjust to the different priorities of international competition. But I, for one, never undervalued his contribution to the team and I've been proved right.

Niall Quinn is a lad I would like to have played more often. At one point, he looked the logical replacement for Frank Stapleton but then Tony Cascarino came back into the squad and Quinn was pushed further down the queue. Yet, I believe that in time he will make his mark with Ireland. He has not developed at the rate which looked likely when he won a Littlewoods Cup medal with Arsenal a couple of years ago but that had a lot to do with the arrival at the club of Alan Smith.

For the next couple of years, the most stable thing in his life was probably his place in the Ireland squad but happily he eventually called it a day at Highbury and moved to Manchester City. I am convinced that, with his height and ability to upset opponents, his time will come and I certainly would have no hesitation in using him if I felt that the pattern of a game needed to be changed in the last 20 minutes or so.

There was a time, frankly, when I thought that David Kelly would not make the cut for Italy. He was struggling with West

Ham early in the season. When I first saw him play with Walsall a couple of seasons ago, I was impressed by his pace, his quickness of thought and the confidence that flows from putting the ball regularly in the net. For some strange reason, those qualities deserted him at Upton Park. With his move to Leicester, however, he is now looking good again and in my opinion he can now go on to justify all the early promise he showed. He is still very fast to the ball and even at times when things are not going his way, he is still prepared to take on defenders. That is the mark of a good player.

Bernie Slaven had scarcely been heard of in Ireland when he set out on the long road to Italy but I think the Irish public sensed that we had uncovered a very useful player when we introduced him for the game with Wales at Lansdowne Road. That was less than 10 weeks ago but, of course, Maurice and I had been aware of him from a long way back. At 29, time is not on his side but with luck, I think he can have two or three good years at the top. He is a good finisher with either foot and while not particularly fast, he generally gets there. As a player who experienced his quota of disappointment early in his career, he has developed a high degree of resilience and that appeals to me. Unlike Scotland, we were prepared to back our judgment with this player and I have a hunch that he will not let us down. Even as I told him that he was coming with us to Italy, I sensed that he realised he was on to the opportunity of a lifetime and that his response would be not less than 100%.

I didn't see John Byrne in action with his club, Le Havre, at any stage of the season but in spite of that, he was always in our thoughts for the World Cup. Pedigree is important at the top level and John had shown enough in the preceding two years to justify his place in the squad. Originally an out-and-out striker, he is now capable of doing an alternative job for us in midfield and in the context of the squad that is important. He shows a lot of skill in getting away from his marker, can produce the inspired pass when it matters and, equally important, he's brave and abrasive in the box. Different players have different roles to discharge in a squad situation but I see Byrne as a valuable 25-minute player, a lad who can come off the bench and give the team a new sense of direction.

Those, then, are the 22 who will carry the Irish flag in Italy. Inevitably, there is disappointment for some. I've already mentioned Gary Waddock, but spare a thought too for the Newcastle players, John Anderson and Liam O'Brien, both of whom have given the team some excellent service in the past.

The one I feel most sympathy for is Tony Galvin. Some people have short memories but I recall Tony doing a magnificent job for us in West Germany when we needed a player to run at defences down the left. Were it not for injury, he might well have filled the same role for us in Italy but sadly his season never really got off the ground at Swindon. It was, I think, typical of Tony that when he was eventually ruled out on medical advice and he realised that his chance of playing in the World Cup finals was gone, probably for ever, he was the first to wish his replacement good luck. That was the mark of a special person and it hurts me to leave him behind.

WEDNESDAY 30
May 1990
●

A bad start to the day. I've got a stomach bug and there is no way I am going to make it to the training ground with the lads. Maurice takes charge and puts them through two hard running sessions. There is a risk of people getting strains and pulls but they need the work to build up their confidence.

The reports on Ronnie Whelan are not encouraging. He has shed a lot of muscle on his leg and he still limps a little when he runs. He has a lot of graft ahead of him if he hopes to make it back in time for the England game. He did plenty of 45-second-interval running and was worked until he got physically sick. That, I imagine, didn't endear either Maurice or me to him but it's got to be done.

Ray Houghton's pelvic strain comes and goes and continues to give cause for concern but I'm less worried about Kevin Moran and David O'Leary, both of whom are getting back into the swing of things after their injuries.

Maurice tells me that he has done a little ball work with the boys at the end of the running sessions—and I understand why. Normally, I don't mix hard physical work with ball practice but we have to take account of the feelings of our two goalkeepers, Paddy Bonner and Gerry Peyton. They would work 24 hours a day if you let them and if they don't get practice, they sulk. So I generally take the diplomatic way out and add on a bit at the end of the session to keep them happy.

Alan McLoughlin arrives in from London and, oddly enough, within an hour or so, I get a call from Gary Waddock. He had asked for permission the previous day to leave the camp and go home and, reluctantly, I agreed. Now, it transpires that he has been approached by an English tabloid to do a piece on me which would obviously be detrimental. He refused and that pleased me no end.

If there is any dirty linen to be washed— and I hope there won't—I don't want it done in public. There was probably a good few quid in it for Gary but to his credit, he kept his silence and refused the money.

THURSDAY 31
May 1990
●

Still not feeling 100% but in the belief that anything is better than staying in my room, I plan to go training. Got a call from some Italian television people saying that they wished to do some pen pictures of the players—the kind of data they show on the screen before and during games.

I reckon it will take half an hour—in fact, it consumes the greater part of three hours and we miss an entire morning's training. I'm furious and when they call me back shortly afterwards to tell me that they have to do it all over again because the camera was knackered in the first instance, they get a two-word reply. They complain to RTE and I receive a phone call from Dublin asking me if I will reconsider. I grudgingly agree—but this time on our conditions when we go training in the afternoon.

Houghton is still wandering about doing nothing and, more ominously, Whelan has pulled a muscle in his thigh. This doesn't surprise me greatly, for when you are recovering from a serious injury you tend to get other related troubles.

I get some interesting mail, including a batch of sheets with the words of the Irish national anthem typed on them in Irish. Some people are offended that when the players are standing to attention facing the flag, they are not seen to be singing the anthem. I take the point—but what can I do? There might be some chance if they gave me the words in English but to ask my lot to sing it in Irish—really!

FRIDAY 1
June 1990

●

The sun was out this morning and we suffered in training. The injuries, I'm afraid, are getting no better and we're now beginning to press on towards our first game. It looks as if there are going to be some difficult decisions to be made.

I took a press conference after training and unfortunately I made a few gaffes. The main contingent of press people has yet to arrive but we still have a fair few Dublin-based writers with us and those who write Irish stories for the English press.

People had predicted that I might have some hassle with journalists on this trip, but so far it has not been the case. Theirs is a hard enough old job for they have to sit around the hotel all day waiting for something to happen. And there is a limit to the number of times they can go on writing about the injury problems of Whelan and the rest.

I help them out as best I can by trying to say something different, express an opinion on issues not immediately related to our squad. There is nothing fundamentally wrong with that. As a national coach, I'm entitled to say my piece on topics which I think may affect my team. Thus, when FIFA issue a threat to send home referees if they don't crack down firmly on violent play, I say my piece. I don't now, and never have, condoned violence on a football field but, as I interpret it, this directive is going to scare referees to the point where somebody making a strong tackle is in danger of being booked.

Tackling is a legitimate part of football and when a player stays within the rules, it is grossly wrong to punish him. Now they're talking about imposing big fines with red and yellow cards and I voice my disagreement through the press.

Fine, but at this stage I realise that I may be getting a reputation at FIFA headquarters for shooting my mouth off. I'd better be more careful in the future. From here on in, I aim to stick as closely as possible to matters relating only to our games.

In choosing that line, I know I won't be doing the news people any favours but the problem is that even on those occasions when I am speaking tongue in cheek they note every word I say and report it accordingly.

For example, we have a game against Malta tomorrow. It is a match I don't particularly want and has been arranged only as a gesture of gratitude to the Maltese FA for putting their facilities at our disposal for training purposes. The last thing I need now, however, is another injury to complicate our problems. I tell the press that this is a game we can afford not to take seriously and to illustrate the point I said that the players can pick the team themselves.

That, of course, was a wild exaggeration but yes, you've guessed it, it is recorded in this morning's papers as fact. The Maltese are not impressed, for statements like that are not exactly designed to attract the local fans through the turnstiles.

We relaxed at the swimming pool in the afternoon and the instruction to players was to take the necessary precautions. A firm has kindly given us oils and creams for sun-tan but even with these, there must be caution. We don't want anybody burning and the orders were for sunbathing periods of not more than an hour initially. The players, under the eye of Mick Byrne and Charlie O'Leary, followed instructions to the letter and soon we can afford to be less vigilant and extend the length of the sessions by the pool.

Tonight we went to the local Labour Party club where the beer is cheap and I'm among my own. But Maurice Setters is like a fish out of water. He is a true blue Conservative and a photograph of him in a place like that could do his image irreparable damage!

Together we took on the Maltese manager, Horst Heese, and a friend of his in a game

of pool—and lost. Horst's mate is a charming man who once had a relationship with Elizabeth Taylor and I'm not surprised that she found him attractive. His pluses playing pool are less obvious and had I been able to see the bloody table properly, I think we might even have won.

SATURDAY 2
June 1990

●

Match day and a lie in for the players. As I said, I didn't want this game but now that it was here, I treated it seriously. Chris Morris, Ronnie Whelan, Ray Houghton and Mick McCarthy were all unavailable but I asked everybody else to strip.

The team had Alan McLoughlin and John Sheridan in central midfield with Niall Quinn up front and, as such, was useful in determining the options available to me later in the event of a crisis.

We went about the job in a workmanlike way and with all due respect to the Maltese I think the scoreline should have read 6–0 instead of 3–0 in our favour. As in Turkey, however, the match officials were so obsessed with the offside rule that most times when we pushed forward we were penalised.

Malta had some good individuals in their team but overall they never threatened after Quinn, who enjoyed a fine game, had put us in front. I brought on Frank Stapleton and Andy Townsend in the second half and they both scored to put a better gloss on our win. Townsend's shot was a superb effort but the goal which really caught the imagination belonged to Stapleton.

Sheridan crossed with his left foot, which surprised me greatly, and Frank, in a situation in which he has few peers, made no mistake with the header. That was his 20th goal in international football and it broke the Irish record which had stood to the name of Don Givens.

I am happy for Frank for it means that his trip is memorable in at least one aspect. Unless things go very much off the rails, I don't hold out much hope of his playing in Italy but for a man who has given such great service to Ireland, it is fitting that he should get the record.

Overall, however, the players who impressed me most were McLoughlin and Sheridan. This was Alan's first senior game for us and even after making allowance for the quality of the opposition, I liked what I saw. He was sharp and authoritative going forward and with a little luck might have scored with his first touch. More than ever, I am now convinced that we have uncovered a fine international player.

Sheridan stepped up considerably on recent displays. He was tackling more effectively, tracking better and I liked the way he picked out Stapleton with the cross for that third goal.

Against that, I was unhappy again with Steve Staunton's contribution at left back. His defensive qualities leave a lot to be desired and too often, it seems to me, he doesn't know whether to stick or to twist. Chris Hughton, by comparison, had another admirable game and is now looking a good player once more.

Generally, it's been a good exercise for us and in spite of the earlier reservations, good for morale.

I have given the lads a night out on the town with few restrictions. In a place like Malta with the emphasis on holidaymakers, that can be tricky but I've given them some advice born of hard experience: don't get involved in hassle; stay in groups; and frequent only those places where there are a lot of people. Above all, I don't want anybody bringing trouble back to the hotel.

Together with Horst Heese, Maurice Setters and James Mossop, an old newspaper friend from my part of the world, I'm off to dinner in the St Julien's Bay area of the city.

SUNDAY 3
June 1990

●

I drank the best part of a bottle of whiskey last night and I bloody well suffered for it this morning. The lads allowed me to have a lie in and Maurice took them training at 11 o'clock to get the booze out of their systems. Generally, a very quiet day.

In the evening, the players skipped a pre-arranged bowling session in Valetta and I went to my room at 10.30 because there was nobody about in the foyer. It is only in these situations when I'm alone and take out my form reports on our first phase opponents that I really worry.

During the day I work with the lads and get on with the hour to hour business but back in the room when I pour myself a whiskey and pull up the chair to watch television, I get to thinking and plotting.

The England game doesn't trouble me unduly. I know their players and they know mine and the game, I feel, is going to follow a certain pattern. But I play out the likely plot of the Egyptian game many times in my mind—even more so, the Dutch match.

In a sense, that's strange. After all, by the time we get to meeting Holland, we may need nothing out of the game to qualify. On the other hand, we may need everything. Who knows? I should be concentrating more on how to get a result against England but it's difficult to stop your thoughts racing away with you.

Coincidentally, Holland's game against Yugoslavia was on the television tonight. Naturally I was interested. They eventually won 2–0 but if I'm honest I've got to say that I was not impressed by what I saw on the screen. If this is their true form, they're not as good as they were. There are a couple of weaknesses in the team which weren't evident when we played them in West Germany.

Koeman at centre back looks as if he has gone off the boil. He is slow on the turn, now having to hold on to opponents to prevent himself being 'skinned'. On this display, he is a racing certainty to pick up a yellow card in the championship. Additionally, they are not nearly as threatening down the flanks—and that gives me hope.

Against that, however, the evidence of my own eyes tells me that Frank Rijkaard now looks an even better player. Marco Van

Basten is sharp and alert up front and in between long spells of mediocrity Ruud Gullit shows some good touches. His is a free role in the team but he stitches it all together for them in a manner which puts him apart from everybody else on the park. The man is moving too easily, reading the game too well, for our peace of mind.

MONDAY 4
June 1990

●

My worst fears are realised when we go training in the Ta'Qali complex at 10.30. Ronnie Whelan now tells me that his thigh muscle is acting up again and I feel as if I've heard it all before.

The problem with any player coming back from a serious injury like his is that you tend to favour the other, sound leg when you run or kick a ball. Very often, however, the cure proves more damaging than the sickness and you end up with two bad legs. Clearly, Whelan has now discovered this and his prospects of recovering in time for the England match look more dodgy than ever.

Steve Staunton is also in a spot of bother with a hamstring strain and doesn't take part in the general training. Maurice takes charge of the session and works the lads till they are ready to drop. We are back to working with the ball this morning and that, obviously, suits the players. Generally, they do the running and exercising bit only with reluctance but the miniature matches are different. Everybody wants to be involved in them.

There are times when Maurice and I close

our eyes and pray while we're watching on the line. These may be only knockabouts but the competitive instincts are still there. Players go into the tackle regardless, and you cringe with apprehension.

I tell them over and over to be more careful but I'm afraid I am not getting through to them. After all, how do you convince Mick McCarthy to forget the habits of a lifetime and pull out of the tackle. I can't and by now, I don't even try.

We go back to the hotel for lunch and then out to relax by the pool. Training, eating and sleeping is the order of the day with eating a clear winner in the popularity stakes. By now, a clear pattern has emerged in the way players spend their leisure time.

I never attempt to organise things for them during the day. There are lots of recreational facilities available like swimming, table tennis, pool and miniature golf but that side of things is best left to themselves.

Playing cards is one of the bigger pastimes and I am interested to discover that there are three kinds of 'schools' catering for the committed, the half-hearted and the novices. The first-named is comprised of Kevin Moran, Kevin Sheedy, Tony Cascarino and John Sheridan. You don't mess about with these lads—they take their game seriously. The 'readers' in the squad are Chris Hughton and Frank Stapleton. Count me in among the crossword addicts.

TUESDAY 5
June 1990

●

A bit of a crisis or rather a misunderstanding. I told the press lads this morning that in my opinion Ronnie Whelan is a very, very doubtful starter for the England game because he has too much to do in too short a time. I told them that we will go on working on the player in the hope of having him ready for the later games but that as I see it, he hasn't a 'prayer' of making it by next Monday.

I never at any stage categorically ruled him out of the match but, of course, the reporters told him that I did and he was furious. He came knocking on the door of my room tonight protesting that if I have excluded him from our plans for the England match I should at least have had the good manners to tell him first.

I informed him that I said nothing of the kind. I repeated that I felt he was losing the race against time for the England game but that if he could prove me wrong in training, I would be first up to shake his hand. That seemed to appease him and he went away a lot happier.

This was the last of our half-days. From now on, until we leave the island, it will be training twice a day. We aim to make the most of it.

I arranged a sight-seeing tour of the island in the afternoon but, annoyingly, the coach never turned up to collect us. I made enquiries and was shocked to discover the reason. This morning, as ever, we treated the bruises and the knocks with ice on the journey back to the hotel. But ice melts and when the driver went to inspect his coach later, he found these pools of water. He accused us of peeing in his bus.

The idea that he would even dream of it hurt but he was adamant. No way would he transport the Irish team again and we had to phone the bus station for a replacement.

WEDNESDAY 6
June 1990

●

Now that the hard physical work is out of the way, we get down to practising our set-piece moves. These have always been an important part of football but never more so than in the modern game.

We have put off this part of our training until we had worked on strength but now it is time to knuckle down to it. It was interesting to note the reaction of players since we resumed our programme of two sessions a day. Some revelled in it; others thought it was too much. But at the end of the day, it wasn't up to them to determine the workload. Maurice and I would decide that and they would obey.

We work on things like providing crosses for Paddy Bonner and Gerry Peyton, giving Tony Cascarino and John Aldridge heading practice in front of goal and rehearsing our free-kick routine like chipping the ball with the inside of the right boot, dipping it over 'walls' and various other ploys.

Back in the hotel, I hear the odd remark by the players like 'We're getting out of jail the day after tomorrow.' They've been here nine days now and it's getting more difficult to

prevent them becoming bored. That is normal and it shows that they are getting increasingly impatient for the real action to start. I remember the feeling well from my own playing days.

Keeping their minds occupied in that situation is hard but we persevere. The main thing is to ensure that when they retire to bed at 10.30, they are tired enough to sleep. Looking at some of the expressions around me, I need not worry too much on that count.

THURSDAY 7
June 1990

●

Another routine day at the office. We've extended the nine-a-side games to 45 minutes and it's doing nothing at all to improve the state of our nerves. I watch the sliding tackles go in and I picture a hundred different injuries. But this is a man's game and I trust that somebody up there is looking after them.

Whelan is now joining in the hard work but still the doubts persist. Normally, I would have ruled him out by now but Ronnie is Ronnie and I've seen him come back from lay-offs of three or four weeks and deliver the goods for Liverpool. He is still a key member of my team and I will not tell him he's gone until I absolutely have to. But deep down, I feel that it is becoming an increasingly lost cause.

When we get back, the hotel manager asks me if he can make some presentations to the players. He likes them. Naturally, I agree and go along with his suggestion that he lay on a bit of a reception with drinks before our evening meal.

Each of the lads goes up to receive a presentation of glassware and when the manager finishes his little speech, they applaud. That gratifies me yet again. I like my players to show respect for other people and the entire staff at the hotel have worked hard to make our stay as comfortable as possible.

In all our time here, they had not had a single complaint to make about our players or any member of the official party. That says it all about a very special squad.

FRIDAY 8
June 1990

●

D-day for Ronnie. We're due to travel to Sardinia later in the day but before we take our leave of Malta, we have an important date at the Ta'Qali complex at 10.30.

We plan to have a fully competitive hour-long game in the sun—the first flat-out test since the match with Malta thirteen days ago. It will tell much about the state of readiness of the team and for Ronnie, it's crucial.

I arrange with Horst Heese to have five members of the Maltese national team play in the game. The purpose is to introduce a little variation into things and the presence of the Maltese will be valuable in our well-rehearsed set-piece ploys.

Jimmy Sirrel fails to show to referee the match, so I decide to take charge. I warn the players that I will blow for frees any

time I see fit for part of the exercise is to practise free taking. Inevitably, most interest focuses on Ronnie and he starts well. Gradually, it becomes apparent however that he is moving at just one pace and that any time he attempts to accelerate he is restricted by that pulled thigh muscle. Finally, after 45 minutes he walks off and then we know that for him there will be no game next Monday. Damn! Whelan has always been central to the structure of our team and here we are about to take on England without him.

The staff at the hotel lined up to see us off and we had a whip-around among the players to show our appreciation of the way they have looked after us.

Whatever else, we know that we will have a group of dedicated Maltese people rooting for us when we get to Italy. After a delayed departure, we soon discovered the first signs of Italian bureaucracy. They want to know the precise time of our arrival and our plans when we reach the hotel. The problem is that we get the same message from six different officials of the local organising committee of Italia '90.

I told them to expect us when they see us but when we set down in Sardinia, there was a small army of policemen, some with dogs, and hordes of media people awaiting us.

A press conference was called and I was surprised to be told that we are one of the last squads to arrive. For me, our timing is just about right. We've done our homework away from the glare of the international media and now we've only three days to contend with the publicity machine before we meet England. As I judge it, that makes sense.

On the way from the airport to the hotel, we had an entourage of outriders, police cars front and back, and a helicopter hovering overhead. It's bizarre: we are only a football team, after all.

The hotel complex, fronting on to a private beach, is fine. Players are housed three to an apartment. I think we're going to like it here.

SATURDAY 9
June 1990

●

We went to the training ground, a 30-minute bus ride from our hotel, in the centre of the city. I held a press conference there, the first of many today.

I will not be naming my team until the mandatory 50 minutes before kick-off deadline on Monday. This doesn't particularly suit me but Bobby Robson has intimated that this was the policy he would adopt. If Bobby wants to play silly buggers, so be it. I have no intention of giving him the drop on us by letting him have our team selection first.

I can't see any justification for this cat and mouse attitude. Neither of us was doing our players any favours. By refusing to go public with our team sheets, we are merely feeding them with additional, useless information on opponents who might not even be involved in the game. I challenged Bobby to call me with his team news and I would let him have mine but of course he refused. I told the press conference all this.

In fact, I was bluffing a bit because I still haven't finalised my side. With Ray Houghton fit again, I have no problems in choosing the midfield line but, as of now, I am still uncertain about my choice of full backs and central defenders.

Mick McCarthy was always going to play—the tester is to decide between Kevin Moran and David O'Leary for the other position in the centre. Both have recovered from knocks and both have convincing claims for selection.

In matters like these, I like to bend the ear of other senior players. McCarthy is going to have to play with the guy I choose and in that situation, his opinion seems relevant. He told me today that he would be happy to go with either player but stressed that he had played more often with Moran and that together they had done the closing down job I had asked them to do. So Moran it was: he was the guy with the track record.

I also sought Mick's opinion and that of Ronnie Whelan on whether I should play Steve Staunton at left back. The lad's form was worrying me for he was lapsing too often into what I would call his Liverpool role, content to fill the hole without making early contact with the opposing winger.

Chris Hughton, by contrast, is playing well. This was a tougher decision than you might think but after talking with the two lads I plumped for Staunton. Hughton can play on either flank if I need him during the game so he is more valuable starting on the bench.

I had a word with Steve later today, told him of my plans but made it quite clear to him that if he didn't do the business,

I would have no hesitation in whipping him off. To emphasise the point, I informed him that I would not confirm his selection until I looked at him in training the following evening.

Back at the hotel there was another round of press conferences—the damn things seem to go on all day. By now, it's becoming a real problem—I will have to sit down and work out an arrangement whereby I will meet all the media people at an appointed time each day and leave it at that.

I then had problems of a different nature when a lady official of FIFA made an appointment to see me and gave me some tickets. I didn't realise that she was talking about tickets for the various dignatories coming from Ireland for the game and she wanted me to advise her on the order of seniority.

To hell with that! I had enough trouble in sorting out a team without deciding which minister should sit where in the stand. Once I copped on, she got short shrift and I left Tony O'Neill to deal with the situation.

That's enough for one day. I need a drink and a night's sleep.

SUNDAY 10
June 1990
●

The calm before the storm. There was an open-air Mass celebrated in the grounds of the hotel and most of the players and officials took part. This was a quiet day with the emphasis on relaxation to get the players in the right frame of mind for the game.

Sunbathing was again reduced to just one hour for while most of the players are by now well tanned, we still cannot afford to take risks with anybody burning. Ray Houghton is beginning to redden too much for our liking and after all the worry we have been through with him, the last thing I want to hear is that he has been affected by the sun.

We went to the town hall in the afternoon where the mayor made a presentation of a replica of the World Cup to the association. Each of the players got a medal to commemorate the occasion. After being cooped up in our hotel for two days, we relished the opportunity to socialise— if only for an hour or so.

That night we went to the stadium at 9 o'clock to familiarise ourselves with the conditions likely to obtain at the same time tomorrow evening. We were pleasantly surprised to discover that after all the dire warnings about heat and humidity, the weather is not wholly dissimilar to the conditions back home.

There was a refreshing breeze blowing, the evening was cool and if things stay like that, neither England nor ourselves will be unduly put out by the conditions. Unlike Bobby Robson the previous evening, we threw our training session open to the public—anybody who so desired could come and watch us work. I reckon we have nothing to hide from anybody.

In fairness, Bobby probably wanted to rehearse his set-piece bits and, as such, it was perfectly reasonable that he should wish to do so behind closed doors. We, on the other hand, had done our thing in Malta and by the time we reached Italy it

Niall Quinn scores against Holland.

The Romanian game in Genoa was like a home match for us, thanks to the fantastic Irish support.

△ The big boys, Quinn and Cascarino, outjump the Romanian defence.

△ Paul McGrath showing what a beautifully balanced runner he is as he takes on the Romanians.

△ Steve Staunton and Iovan Sabau.

△ Ray Houghton gets stuck in.

△ The scene just before the penalty shoot out against Romania.

Packie Bonner saves Timofte's penalty. What a moment!

Before and after. David O'Leary kept his cool and saw us into the quarter finals. And the lads let him know what they thought of him!

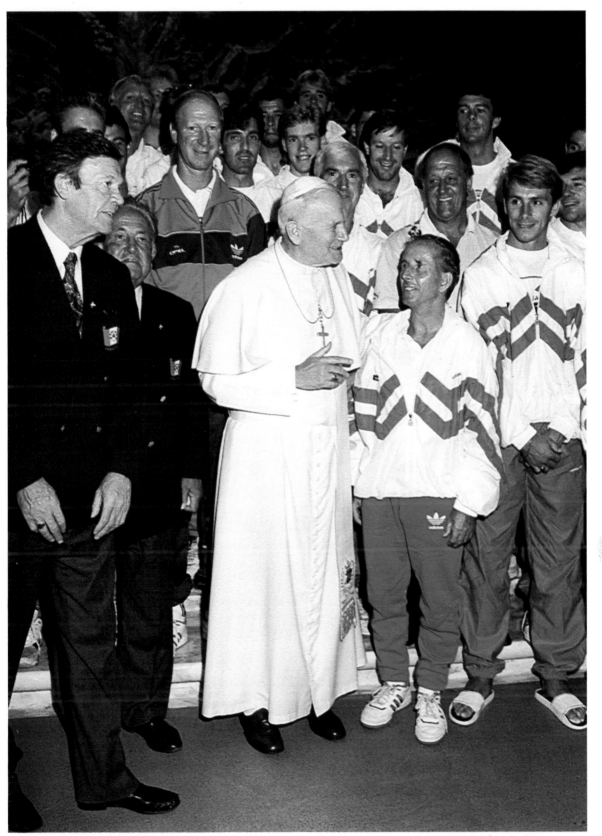

△ One of the most memorable occasions on the whole trip was the morning we were received by His Holiness the Pope.

Whatever about feeling at home in Genoa, we knew we were away from home in Rome's Olympic Stadium for the quarter-final clash with Italy.

△ Paul McGrath and Giannini.

Mick McCarthy and Paul McGrath both played superbly against Italy. Here they challenge Serena (above) and Giannini.

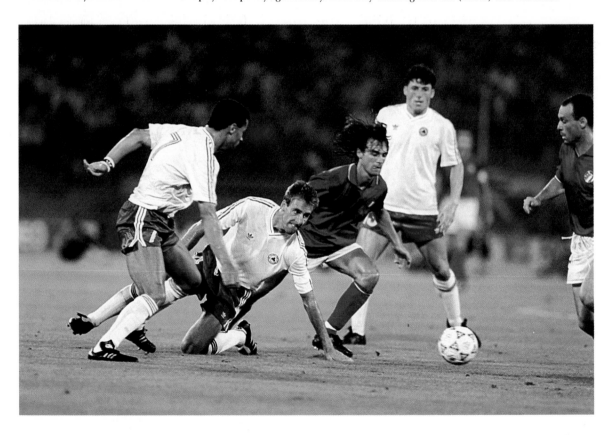

△ The brilliant 'Toto' Schillaci after he has scored the goal that ended our World Cup dream.

△ Saluting the fans in Rome. If I looked glum, it's because that's how I felt. It's never good to lose and this Irish team just isn't used to it.

What a homecoming! What supporters!

△ Kevin Moran shows the flag.

was merely a question of keeping the lads supple.

We didn't do any serious work. The purpose of the visit was to look at the lights, examine the playing surface and generally, get a picture of the place fixed in our minds. We liked what we saw—there can be no excuses about the pitch if we lose.

Before we left, I called out my team selection to the players and, inevitably, it was received with delight by some and disappointment by others. I could well understand the feelings of both the satisfied and the aggrieved but there is a big job of work to be done and sentiment cannot be allowed to enter into the equation.

MONDAY 11
June 1990
●

We had a late breakfast and then went for a bit of a walk on the roads around our hotel. This is traditional with us on match days for I find it is easier to have a few private words with individuals while we are rambling than I would, say, in the lounge of the hotel.

We then had a light lunch and went to bed to rest up. Amazingly, given the nature of our date that evening, I slept soundly for a couple of hours before being awakened by the 5 o'clock call. After a cup of tea and a slice of toast, we left with a police escort for the stadium 2½ hours before the kick-off.

There is a set pattern we follow on the journeys to games and given the composition of our team, it may surprise you. We play Irish rebel songs on the coach ride and at the designated time, just as we approach the stadium, Charlie O'Leary puts on a tape of 'Sean South of Garryowen'.

That's the kind of stuff that raises the blood temperature and as we swept into the stadium for a meeting with England, it now sounded more appropriate than ever.

Inside, we discovered that the England squad had already arrived. At that stage, of course, we still didn't know the make-up of their team but once the players started greeting each other, the bits and pieces quickly fell into place.

The first English player I met was Steve McMahon. After a couple of seconds, I discovered that he wasn't playing and that, almost certainly meant that Paul Gascoigne was in the team. It surprised me just a little. Paul is one of the most gifted midfielders in Britain but somehow I felt that this wouldn't be his type of game. Bobby Robson, I suspected, wouldn't risk him being roughed out of it. But I was wrong.

Gradually, as the players came back in after talking to each other, the format of the two teams emerged and before Bobby and I went public, we both knew exactly what we faced. So much for secrecy and the 50-minute deadline.

Out in the stadium, conditions were a long way removed from what we had been led to believe. It was windy, there was a lot of cloud about and, if anything, it was on the cool side. In short, it was an evening borrowed from April in Ireland.

Now that we knew for certain the formation of the England team, we could get down to discussing the opposition in detail and for 20 minutes or so, I went through the things which pleased me in their team—and those which could hassle us. The first plus was Bobby's choice of Bryan Robson—I desperately wanted him to play.

There was a time when Bryan was one of the greats but not any more. We had handled him well in the European championship and I had seen nothing in the intervening period to suggest that he had halted his decline. The fact that he was now playing alongside Gascoigne delighted me for I was certain that Bobby just didn't have enough competitors in midfield to win that particular battle.

We would encourage Gascoigne to play in the area between his back four and the half-way line. Once he gets over half-way, he can be dangerous for his final pass is terrific. It was up to our midfielders to ensure that they got stuck in for with players of the quality of Gascoigne, Chris Waddle and John Barnes in their team, the last thing we wanted was to allow England to settle on the ball.

Maurice Setters looked at their team and said that they were going to have a go at our full backs. I said fine for I believed that we could live with that situation as long as Morris and Staunton stuck close to Barnes and Waddle.

I pointed out to them that Waddle and, to a lesser extent, Barnes will not normally run behind the full back. They want the ball played to their feet to take him on. It was up to Morris and Staunton to stay tight on them until they manoeuvred them into a position where our wing halves could pick them up. Then they could drop off.

I talked about Gary Lineker and Peter Beardsley. I have this conviction about Peter that he will not go into the box, not follow things into the six-yards area. Instead, he will hang about on the fringe of the penalty area, usually on the left, waiting for the ball to be knocked out by a defender. When that happens, it is vital to go to him immediately. If the defender hesitates, Beardsley will run at him and generally 'skin' him. But Peter gets confused when confronted quickly and forced to go in the direction he doesn't want.

Lineker, I pointed out, has tremendous speed when racing on to the ball played over the top and it was again down to our midfield to ensure that the threat was cut off at source. At the other end, we would encourage England to build, as they always did, slowly.

When Peter Shilton throws the ball to either his full backs or centre backs, encourage it. Encourage him to feel comfortable. Don't stand too far back but don't get too close to them either. Make them feel easy on the ball when they play it across the back four and then pounce. Armed with that kind of advice, I believed our players had the ability to do the job I wanted.

We played with the wind in the first half and had made most of the running when England scored in virtually their first attack after only nine minutes. Kevin Sheedy, thinking the ball was going to run over the sideline, stoppped running. It was a fatal error.

I was surprised when Bobby Robson selected Paul Gascoigne for the game in Cagliari. He played well, but I think we had the measure of him. Here he is in a spot of bother with Chris Morris!

Andy Townsend did a fine job in marking Gascoigne. Here they tussle for a loose ball in midfield, watched by Paul McGrath.

After being one-nil down to England for so long, this was the moment we had waited for. Steve Staunton, Kevin Sheedy,
Kevin Moran, Tony Cascarino and Alan McLoughlin celebrate Sheedy's equaliser in Cagliari.

Waddle, reacting quickly, got it, turned, looked up and hit this cracking centre into the penalty area. Lineker, who had originally taken up a near-post position, cleverly peeled off and as the cross came in, McCarthy couldn't make up his mind whether to attack it or go to Gary.

He did neither and Lineker, doing well to control the ball, albeit with his shoulder, wrongfooted Bonner before running the ball in. Most people blamed Mick for the goal but as I saw it, it was Morris who blundered more. Instead of taking up a cover position inside Lineker, he was caught square and with Gary about, you normally pay for mistakes like that.

That was a bad start but I still believed we could retrieve the game. Unfortunately, the wind proved more of a hindrance than a help for it meant that the long balls aimed at Tony Cascarino, were carried that yard or so too long.

England, as I reminded the lads during the half-time break, would have to cope with the same problem in the second half but even as I spoke, an electrical storm was breaking over the ground. The wind dropped but now we had heavy rain and it meant that the ball would skid on a fast pitch.

It was an added challenge for both teams but I told our fellows that if they kept their shape, we would get our reward. To be honest, there were times when I doubted it for in spite of all the pressure—and we were still taking the game to England in the second half—the ball never ran for us.

Then came two significant developments. I took off John Aldridge, pushed Ray

Houghton a little more forward and brought Alan McLoughlin into midfield. The reasoning was that the game needed a change of direction and I reckoned that by running at England from midfield, we would unsettle a defence which was then beginning to play with confidence.

Bobby Robson immediately countered that move by sending on Steve McMahon, presumably to combat McLoughlin's aggressive running. But it never worked out like that. McMahon positioned himself just in front of his back four whereas the real need for England at that time was to start competing in midfield and prevent us from getting at their defence.

As it happened, McMahon was only on the pitch a couple of minutes when he was centrally involved in our equaliser. After winning the ball, he gave it back to Kevin Sheedy and Sheedy, superb in such situations, swept the angled left-footed shot into the corner of the net.

McMahon took some stick from the press afterwards but his, I thought, was a pressurised mistake. We put people under pressure and it was no accident of fortune that Sheedy should profit from it. We each had a couple of chances subsequently but in the end the 1–1 scoreline was fair.

At the post-match press conference, I was amused to hear Bobby Robson's comments that England had the game won and threw it away. That was rubbish. They were never in control of the game, even after leading for so long. Their claim that they should have had a penalty when Waddle fell in the area, was also rubbish.

We took out of the match only what we deserved. Above all else, we could not afford to be beaten and of course the point was very welcome.

Back at the hotel, there were telex and fax messages from Charlie Haughey, Alan Dukes, members of the hierarchy and a couple of fishing organisations offering me free fishing. Now we are going to have a few quiet drinks, a bit of chat and then early to bed.

We leave for Palermo at seven in the morning.

THURSDAY 14
June 1990

●

Life in Palermo is taking time to settle. We go training in the morning but really the talk has less to do with football than the hotel which will be home to us for the next week. In a nutshell, it's not measuring up to expectations and the players are not slow to let us know.

In a sense, we were spoiled by our location in Sardinia. After all it's not every hotel which has its own private beach and sufficient facilities to cater for most tastes. Maurice Setters chose our headquarters in Sicily when he visited the island earlier in the year and he did so on the premise that it was sufficiently far from the centre of Palermo to minimise the possibility of the squad being upset by supporters dropping in at inconvenient times.

In that, he was absolutely right. The most charitable comment I can pass on the place is that it is spectacularly lonely. The hotel seems to be miles from anywhere, there is no place to go and the rooms are pitifully small. Moreover, we had a problem at first

with the way the food was being prepared. Eventually, Eddie Corcoran was delegated to liaise with the people in the kitchen and this turned out to be a shrewd move. Eddie, something of a specialist in this area, got the whole problem of menus sorted out and soon the complaints about under-cooked food and too much greasy food disappeared.

In my room tonight, I got to worrying again about the Egyptian team and the problems they are likely to give us in our game next Sunday. Maurice and I watched them draw 1–1 with Holland in Palermo two days ago and we were impressed by much of what we saw. True, the Dutch gave them a lot of room in which to play but the Egyptians still won a lot of the neutral support by the way in which they mixed the naive with the preposterous.

At times, they could be stunning in their use of the ball. On other occasions, they committed basic mistakes in the top third of the field. But the manner in which the boy 'fell' for the penalty which would eventually earn them a 1–1 draw showed that, in terms of theatrics and the ability to influence referees, they had nothing to learn from European players. Additionally, their defenders had this knack of getting the merest touch on the ball to deflect it out of the path of the opposition. Technically, they were still suspect but any team which could get players as quickly behind the ball as they did merited respect.

Three months ago, I travelled to Cairo to watch them in one of their build-up games and I remember being quoted as saying that they were a very ordinary lot.

In fact, I said nothing of the kind. What I did predict was that our style would cause them a lot more problems than either the English or the Dutch. I hope to God I'm right!

FRIDAY 15
June 1990

●

We take a run into town to see the stadium in Palermo and are impressed. It has all the attributes of a modern stadium and the back drop of a cliff face, rising sheer into the sky, is something else. I wonder to myself how the Irish fans will set the place alight with their colour and their songs in two days' time.

Reports are beginning to reach us of the reaction back home to the 1–1 draw with England. We hear of thousands of people out on the streets, singing and dancing, and that amuses us just a little. The Irish, apparently, have always had an inferiority 'thing' in their football meetings with the English. But we've long since reached the point where we knocked that on the head. If we played them every day of the week, we'd expect to get a good result every time.

To that extent, the scoreline in Cagliari was no great cause for national celebration but it just went to prove that old traditions die hard. Put another way, the expectations of the team and its supporters are not always as one.

Now the Egyptian game may be slightly different. Pedigree, performance and almost anything else you care to mention, suggests that we should win. But I have

this premonition that it's going to be a lot more difficult than many expect. Yet, dammit, we should be capable of putting at least one past them. And unless something awful happens, they're surely not going to score against us.

The media people are with us as usual when we get back to the hotel. And, inevitably, they all want to know about my plans for Ronnie Whelan and if I'm going to play him. This amazes me, just as much as it irritates. I tell them that Ronnie is working hard in training but they seem to miss the point that it is now ten weeks since he last played a game.

I've already made it clear that I regard Whelan, fit and in form, as a key member of my team. I've also referred to the fact that in the past Ronnie has come back from injury to deliver the goods for Liverpool. But English First Division football is one thing. This is the World Cup and nobody, not even a player of his special talent, can expect to get through a game at this level without a period of reacclimatisation.

No, Whelan won't play on Sunday. I will not announce the team for another 24 hours but I've already decided that it will be unchanged, with precisely the same substitutes, from that which played England. It's not going to endear me to Ronnie's pals but hell, I'll go with what I believe in. We took the game to England—now we'll do the same against Egypt.

It is traditional on these occasions for Opel to organise a 'press night' for the various journalists with the team. The entourage gets bigger from one year to the next and this one in the Terrasini area of the city threatens to be the most raucous yet. Maurice and I set off to attend but in fact, we never get there.

On the way to Terrasini, we are waylaid by three or four hundred Irish supporters in the main square in the city. A few pints are in order, a nice little girl is brought on to sing to the fans and three hours later, we decide it's too late to attend the press function. Somehow I think we made the right choice.

SATURDAY 16
June 1990

●

Up early and the sense of premonition is still with me. I walk around the hotel, such as it is, and just wonder if the smile will still be on our faces when we get back after tomorrow's game. If we win, we'll have three points in the bag and that ought to be enough to see us through to the second phase of the championship, irrespective of what happens in our final qualifying game against Holland.

Rightly or wrongly, I've convinced myself that it will work out like that. We'll get our two points from Egypt and we'll need nothing from the Dutch when we get to meet them. All very cosy but what happens if the worst comes to the worst and we need a win against Holland to go through? Bloody hell!

The Egyptian match will be played in the afternoon and remembering our experience in West Germany two years ago, that also worries me. But I console myself with the thought that nobody, not even the

Egyptians, relishes the idea of playing football under a hot sun. And given that they don't normally play their games until the late evening, I convince our players that after our long preparation, we'll be actually better equipped than the Egyptians to handle the conditions. I didn't want to dig too deeply into the psychology of that. But it sounds a good line.

We had arranged to go to the stadium at five o'clock, match time, and the instructions were for players to take it easy. I just wanted them to walk around, examine the texture of the grass, get a mental 'fix' on the place. I then told them the team and as I suspected, it didn't greatly please Ronnie Whelan.

I first noticed his annoyance when during a kick-about, I saw him 'hump' a ball into the top deck of the stand. I said to Maurice, 'What's he gone and done that for?' and he told me that Ronnie was annoyed with my team selection. My reaction to that is to instruct Maurice to go and push him a bit harder in training but he's back in a couple of minutes to inform me that Whelan doesn't want to train. Instead, he chose to do some light jogging with Noel King.

Somebody suggested that I should go and talk to him but I wasn't having that. At that moment, I didn't feel any responsibility to explain my decision to him—I would do that when it suited me. For the present, he could fret it out and stew in his own juice.

Subsequently, I heard reports, all 'authentic', of course, of a bust-up between Ronnie and myself, in which blows are alleged to have been exchanged. Nothing could be further from the truth.

Around midnight, Maurice Setters, Noel King, Maurice Price and myself were sitting in the lounge of the hotel when I suddenly noticed Whelan walking about. That annoyed me but then it was explained that he couldn't get to sleep and on the basis that it was better that he come downstairs rather than upset his room-mate, Steve Staunton, I accepted that he had done the right thing.

Clearly, he had something on his mind and eventually he came across and asked if he could have a word in private. I said nay—we'll sit down and anything that has to be said will be said openly. He told me that he couldn't understand my selection—that he felt he was at least deserving of a place on the bench.
I probably shattered him by telling him that the thought never entered my head.

I've watched him carefully, very carefully, in training but he's just not up to it yet. It may be different in a couple of days' time, but just now I'm not prepared to put the team at risk by giving him even a limited role. I reminded him that the strength of our team is our work rate in midfield and that we cannot afford to carry passengers. I desperately want the Ronnie Whelan of old in my team but I'm certainly not prepared to put him in so that he can say that he's played in the World Cup finals.

He wasn't convinced. He just stood there for a minute saying nothing, then turned and went.

SUNDAY 17
June 1990

●

To Ronnie's credit, he was back in training this morning, working harder than ever. The normal tensions which exist between players and those who select teams had produced a delicate problem, but I am glad to have it out of the way.

We made a late start to what was going to be an unusually long day for us. There was a light lunch arranged for 12 o'clock, then off to bed for a rest before leaving to be in the stadium the mandatory 90 minutes before kick-off time.

On my way into the ground I met my brother Gordon who reminded me that I had promised him six tickets for the game. I must have had a drink or two in then, for like the players, I get just two tickets for each match. I go hunting for more, eventually get them and pray that the rest of my problems will be solved just as readily.

Would they what? From the first minutes of the game, I sensed that my worst fears were about to be realised and that anything we got out of the game would have to be achieved the hard way. We pressed them from the kick-off but when it came to attack, the Egyptians simply didn't want to know. You could count on the fingers of one hand the number of times they crossed the half-way line and even then, they were not prepared to push more than two players forward.

The thing to do was to vary our tactics to open up their defence but that was easier said than done. When we played the ball into the corner there were usually three of them surrounding it and when the ball was eventually crossed there were so many bodies in the box that it wasn't funny. It needed a genius to play one-twos through a defence like that and we didn't have one.

The only way to break them down, I felt, was to go, like the Dutch, to the far post but our crossing in the game was woeful. We never once put them under pressure at the far upright and that, for me, was the most disappointing feature of the game. Another irritant was the manner in which the Egyptians wasted time—and were allowed by the referee to get away with it.

They simply refused to retrieve the ball when it went out of play and some of the antics of their goalkeeper, Shobeir, were disgraceful. I reckon that he alone was responsible for killing at least ten minutes of the game and while he was eventually 'booked' for the offence, it was far too late at that point to have any real effect.

Overall, I reckoned that the performance of the referee was dismal. In order to stop Shobeir kicking the ball off his left foot, we delegated John Aldridge to stand on that side of him and the result, on occasions, was that the goalkeeper took as many as 14 or 15 paces with the ball instead of the permitted four. Then when Shobeir, in sheer frustration, dived straight into John, he gave a free out. Incredible!

There was also an occasion I felt when we should have had a penalty after Kevin Sheedy, bursting through, was tripped from behind. In any other area of the pitch, the referee would surely have blown for a free but because Sheedy was in the 'box' at the time he took the easy option.

Overall, we didn't play well or weren't allowed to play well. The ball never once dropped kindly for us in situations in which Cascarino, operating out at the edge of the 18 yards area, had won it cleanly but we still had a couple of opportunities to make the Egyptians pay.

Kevin Sheedy, forced to take the volley high, poked one straight at Shobeir but the best chance of all fell to Ray Houghton, late in the game, when Sheedy's pass put him through on his right foot. The ball to the far post would almost certainly have been a winner, but for some reason best known to himself, he chose the narrow angle and the 'keeper saved. On the day, we desperately needed the Liam Brady of yesteryear or, perhaps, a fit Ronnie Whelan to sort out the final ball for us.

I was furious not just with the blank scoreline but with the way in which Egypt had approached the game. On my way over for the press and television interviews, I thought about doing the diplomatic thing, making excuses for them and praising the way in which they defended.

But I said, bugger it, I'll call it as I saw it. The Egyptians, I said, had adopted a diabolical approach to the game and had reflected no credit on anybody. A team which failed to create a single chance in 90 minutes of football just didn't deserve to be let down lightly.

I hadn't shaken hands with any of the Egyptians after the game—in fairness, they didn't go out of their way to shake mine—and I realised that my post-match

This was me during the Egyptian match. Charlie O'Leary looks like he doesn't know what I am going to do next! I have never been so frustrated. The Egyptians simply didn't come to play football.

△ 'Honest Boss, we tried our best.' Tony Cascarino and me after the Egypt match.

△ Like everyone else, I felt a bit down after the draw against Egypt. I wasn't sorry to get out of the stadium.

comments wouldn't win me any new friends in Cairo. But there are times when one must be brutally honest.

Egypt may have salvaged the point they set out to get but the manner of its achievement brought no credit to the game. From our point of view, the loss of a point, coupled with England's scoreless draw against Holland in Cagliari last night, leaves the group in a dangerous state.

MONDAY 18
June 1990

●

We declare this a rest day, the first we've had since we left Dublin twenty-four days ago. The players' wives and girl-friends were invited to stay in the hotel last night—and some of the kiddies came too. The hotel is off-limits to the press today—it's a time when we just want to relax and be with our loved ones.

The behaviour of everybody in the squad has been exemplary, but there comes a time when it is necessary to relax discipline and get back to more homely values. By six o'clock in the afternoon, however, the last of the wives has left the hotel. Pat has returned to the other side of the island and we're back to the urgent priorities of the football world once more. England had broken with tradition to employ a 'sweeper' in their game with the Dutch and, by all accounts, it worked a charm.

Naturally, the talk got round to our taking a leaf out of Bobby Robson's book and going with an extra defender for our game on Thursday. It's a system we have always scorned in the Irish camp for we

prefer to play our sweeper in front of the back four rather than behind them. Normally a 'libero' operating behind the two centre backs should give you more stability but it doesn't always solve your problems. For one thing, it means that you must spread your midfield cover more widely and in a match plan like ours that could be disastrous.

Maurice and I talked it over for an hour or so and decided that we would look at the plan in operation when we went training the following day. This evening, a Yugoslav friend of ours, an old football acquaintance, took us out to dinner in one of the more fashionable areas of the city. I have never been to a place where security was so visible for there were police and police cars everywhere. We learned afterwards that the annual get-together of the local magistrates was taking place in the same hotel and given the fact that we were in Sicily, the elaborate security measures probably weren't 'over the top'.

TUESDAY 19
June 1990

●

We decided to bring the training session back to the morning. In fact, we never work particularly hard coming up to a game and we'll stay with that pattern now. But, as arranged, we'll drop one of our midfield players from the system and take a look at David O'Leary as a sweeper in our practice game. Ray Houghton will play in midfield for the first quarter with Kevin Sheedy replacing him for the second session.

O'Leary looks comfortable enough, but I'm not happy with what I see. Far from tightening things, the new arrangement creates a situation in which there is more room to attack us down the channels with the two full backs drawn in and up. People are running us down towards the corner flags and the three central defenders look vulnerable. I decide to abandon the experiment at half-time and I think everybody is relieved.

Someday, we may get around to employing a sweeper but we'll do it in our own good time and when we judge that it is right for the team. But to change now, when we don't really know what we're at, would be tantamount to football suicide and so we go back to what we do best. In the second half of the practice game, we look a lot more comfortable and I know for certain that David O'Leary will not be starting the game against Holland.

The other point which concerns me this morning is Tony Cascarino's loss of form. This may be only a practice but Tony has already missed four good chances with his head and it confirms what I've suspected these last couple of days—the lad's confidence is gone. Against Egypt, he was coming to 'show' for the ball out at the edge of the penalty area, whereas I needed him to pounce at the post. I took him aside, told him what I wanted but to no avail. I said, 'I can tell you what to do, advise you of the positions to take up but I can't bloody well do it for you. That bit you must sort out for yourself.'

I stuck it for another five minutes, Cassy didn't improve and, eventually, I was left with no option but to ask him to change places with Niall Quinn. Things picked up immediately, the team got back its shape and Niall looked both comfortable and convincing on the ball.

I went back to the hotel and thought long and hard on what I had just seen but already the team is beginning to form in my mind. Quinn looked infinitely sharper than Cascarino and that will have to be reflected in my selection tomorrow.

David Kelly, yet to play in the championship, also looked quite sharp in training today but then, I saw nothing wrong in the way John Aldridge had moved. This will be a delicate decision to make and I am going to sleep on it.

WEDNESDAY 20
June 1990

●

By now, we're beginning to hear reaction to Sunday's game against Egypt. Strangely, we get very few Irish papers out on this trip. That contrasts sharply with the situation in Germany two years ago when they were on general sale to the public. In a sense, it helped to pull all the fans together during the European championship finals and we are missing that in Italy.

The only papers that are usually available to us are the English tabloids and they don't please me greatly. Nobody needed to remind us of the disappointment of the Egyptian game but when I pick up this tabloid and see the headline 'Jack-Ass' screaming at me, I see red.

In a way, though, I expected nothing different from them. But what really appalled me were the reports reaching me from Dublin that Eamon Dunphy had gone over the top on television when commenting on our display against Egypt. He had apparently said that we were a disgrace and that our performance was a load of rubbish.

Dunphy is a man whose views on football hold no relevance whatsoever for me. Normally, I would dismiss him for what he is, but today I allowed him, unwisely, to get to me. When the bus pulled up in front of the stadium to drop the lads off for training, there was Dunphy and this little guy in a green shirt, who I later discovered was his mate, stationed in a position where they couldn't avoid being seen. Mick McCarthy taps me on the shoulder and says, 'Have you seen who's here?' I advise him to put on his best face and smile.

Training finished, I walk across to the press centre to meet the journalists and one of the first people into the place is Dunphy. Within minutes, he opens his mouth to say something. I chop him. He asks why I won't answer his questions and I tell him that I don't consider that he is a proper journalist. Whereupon the other little fellow in the green shirt pops up on the far side of the room and starts complaining about my attitude.

He tells me he is a colleague of Dunphy's and that he is entitled to a hearing. I advise him that if he wants this press conference to continue, he should take his mate outside. He refuses, so I get up and leave.

In retrospect, that was a mistake. What I ought to have done was to have listened to his questions and then ignored them. All I succeeded in doing was promoting Dunphy—and that hurt.

Before leaving, I told the senior journalists present that I would be happy to talk with them back at the team hotel.

Later, I read that the Dutch camp has called in a faith healer in a desperate attempt to counter the loss of form suffered by players of the quality of Ruud Gullit, Marco Van Basten, Frank Rijkaard and Ronald Koeman. I watched Gullit in some of his earlier games and, to me at least, there were ominous signs that he was coming back to form. The man had been through a harrowing season but now, at last, there are signs that it is all beginning to fit into place for him once more.

Van Basten and Rijkaard have both enjoyed enormously successful seasons with AC Milan and there is just a hint that they have gone stale. But no less than Gullit, they still represent a huge threat if the mood takes them.

This afternoon, Gullit, a fine person, was gracious enough to say some kind things about the Irish team. I know he meant it. He realised that it had been a tight squeak for the Dutch in Gelsenkirchen in 1988 and nothing had happened in the intervening period to suggest that it would be any easier for them now.

Additionally, Leo Beenhakker, their new manager, is at pains to stress that our style would cause them problems. Beenhakker is a man under intense pressure and to me, has the ring of a person already formulating excuses in case things go wrong. It confirms that the Dutch are feeling the pressure every bit as much as we are.

Because of the results of the games to date, Group F has become the most fiercely competitive of all the six sections of the World Cup finals. Not only have the four teams involved got identical points totals but the goals columns are precisely the same.

Going into the last two games there is still everything to play for with the growing possibility of that situation being maintained right to the finish. If it finishes up like that, one team will be balloted out of the championship.

That would be the unkindest cut of all and the Dutch, no less than ourselves, are acutely aware of the position as we prepare for the showdown in Palermo. There could not, therefore, have been a more tense build-up to this game. We have waited two years to avenge ourselves on the Dutch but none of us could have foreseen that the stakes would be quite so high.

THURSDAY 21
June 1990

●

Today's the day. If we get the result we want, we're through to the second phase of the championship. If not, it's back to Dublin for us tomorrow.

I inform the press that I don't want to see them around our hotel before the game. The team will be announced at 10 a.m. and sure enough, the bloody phone never stops ringing after that. I decide to leave

out Cascarino and bring in Niall Quinn up front. The rest of the side will be unchanged. But I name Ronnie Whelan among the substitutes. I bet that will please somebody.

It's another sizzling day—I'm doubly glad now that we're kicking off in the evening—and the usual instructions on sunbathing and the use of headwear apply. In that situation, I am absolutely amazed when I discover that two players have stepped out of line.

The two Maurices and myself are sitting out in the grounds of the hotel around lunch-time when, to my astonishment, I see Frank Stapleton and John Byrne pulling into the little harbour alongside, in a boat. Both are bare chested and neither is wearing a hat. I see red and ask them what the hell they're playing at. They know the rules and they've just gone and thumbed their noses at them. Frank slinks off but John Byrne comes back shortly afterwards to tell me I'm out of order. The way he reads it, they've done nothing wrong—they're not playing that night and they're not even on the bench.

That only makes me more angry. I tell them that they are our responsibility on this trip and I want to be aware of their whereabouts at any given minute of the day or night. I remind them that we're all in this together—what one does, everybody does. The excuse about not playing or not being on the bench doesn't wash with me. What happens if one of the sixteen chosen gets a tummy bug or stubs a toe before the game? It's a disappointing start to the day and it's added hassle. I could have done without it.

The usual routine applied after that. We had a rest, changed into our warm-up gear in the hotel and were soon on our way to the stadium. Even by Irish standards—and the support since we arrived has, as ever, been tremendous—this is something special. There seem to be hundreds of buses on the roads leading to the stadium and the area in the immediate vicinity of the ground is awash with green and orange.

There are a lot of security people around too, presumably because of the reputation of some of the Dutch supporters. But if there is violence in the city today, it is not apparent to us. The good humour of the crowd is unmistakable—I wonder which of the two sets of supporters will be happier at the end of the day. Ninety minutes is a long time to kill when you arrive in the stadium. But on this occasion, at least, I'm determined that the warming-up exercises will be reduced to the minimum.

It's very hot out there and the players will burn up enough energy in the game without the added imposition of an over-rigorous preparation. Our two goalkeepers will listen to nobody in these matters, but I decide to keep a strict eye on the rest and call them in early. Then, after a cold shower, we get to talking about the Dutch, their strengths and their weaknesses.

Ironically, just as we're going in, the Dutch lads are coming out on to the pitch to limber up and we exchange greetings with people like Gullit, Van Basten and the goalkeeper Hans Van Breukelen who at one time played for Notts Forest. Van Breukelen is a nice lad and he expressed the opinion as we passed, that it was going to be another hard game with a similar scoreline as at Gelsenkirchen. Pointing to the sky, I told him that things had now changed and because of the evening start, they were going to find it even more difficult this time. He just smiled.

I shook hands with Leo Beenhakker who looked drawn and tense. I asked him, jokingly, for a ciggy and when he reached into his pocket to get me one, I told him to hang on to it until the end of the game. Come to think of it now, that was one cigarette I never did collect.

Inside the dressing room, behind closed doors, we go through the pre-match drill of analysing the opposition. We now know that Gullit will be operating from a loose midfield base and that means that he will be going down the channels, left and right. When Van Basten drifts into midfield, Ruud will start to run and I want him picked up as he comes away. On no account must he be allowed spin on the ball. If Mick McCarthy goes with him, Paul McGrath will fill the hole at the back.

Chris Morris and Steve Staunton are to close up tight, Pakie is to stay alert and on those occasions when Niall Quinn splits to the right, I want John Aldridge moving to the opposite side of the penalty area with Andy Townsend, hopefully, getting forward to fill the space in the middle.

I tell them to cool down and as usual, the last line in the team talk is, 'Remember, this game is played with the head rather than the heart.' Then I advise them to have a little quiet think about it until the referee comes knocking on the door for them. By the time we get into the tunnel, the lads are all fired up—and then I look at the

Dutch. They're scarcely uttering a word and the tension on their faces is unmistakable. I like that.

Out in the stadium, the scenes which greet us are marvellous. There must be 20,000 Irish supporters in the ground and they're in good voice. Down at the other end of the arena, the place is one vast canvas of orange—and they're giving the Irish a run for it in terms of chanting. Our players have already made it clear that when the National Anthem is being played, they intend to turn around to face the Tricolour on the opposite side of the ground rather than comply with the FIFA directive of looking straight ahead into the box containing the various dignataries at the game. If that's what the players want to do, it's fine by me.

They played our anthem first and the singing from where I stood, was unbelievable. As usual, the band finished well ahead of them but suddenly there was this vast chorus of 20,000 singing unaccompanied and the effect was magic. Then it was the Dutch fans' turn and their performance was no less inspiring. This is what sport is all about—these are the kind of scenes which should make us all proud to be part of football.

Straight from the kick-off, it was obvious that this was going to be another hard game against a team we feared more than most. Gullit looked sharp and fit. Holland were spreading the ball around as only they can and we were having to work damned hard just to keep a hold on them.

Yet, I feel that we are beginning to play our way into the game when we go a goal down after only nine minutes. They get a free kick just outside the area, Gullit runs away from the pack and when the ball is pushed through to him, he plays a one-two with Van Basten and before anybody realises what's happening, it's in the net.

I kick Charlie O'Leary's bag in frustration for we've just given away the simplest of scores and now, more than ever, it's all uphill for us. Time out of number, I had warned them that they must always be alert in those situations, always wary of the unexpected and yet we'd just been caught as square as a barn door. When Gullit ran, somebody should have gone with him! Instead there was this little gap of a yard or a yard and a half as the ball was played through to him and like the great player he is, he took full advantage.

I refused to blame anybody individually, although Kevin Moran was closest to him, but collectively, they all stood indicted. I think Moran and Staunton could both have tackled him but had they stuck their foot in, it would almost certainly have resulted in a penalty. No, the real damage was done seconds earlier.

Give them their due, the Irish players responded admirably to that challenge, and instead of being overrun as we might have been after conceding such a simple goal so early in the game, they put their heads down and battled. Gullit might have had a second goal subsequently, when he headed over after a ball had been played through to him, in space, but the only other moment of alarm I recall was when the big lad, Ronald Koeman, came upfield to test Bonner with a shot from all of 35 yards.

We, for our part, were putting a fair bit of pressure on them with John Aldridge right in the thick of the action. Aldo had the ball in the net from a superb header only to have it disallowed for a hairline offside decision and then, he might have had a penalty when he appeared to be 'taken' from behind. I didn't see the incident clearly. But people who were watching at that end of the ground had no doubt that he'd been fouled.

Half-time found us still 1–0 down and I was still seething over the goal. Nevertheless, the priority now was to get it back. The big need, as I saw it, was to get at their back four more often and with this in mind I told Chris and Steve to get down the flanks at every opportunity. Niall Quinn, I thought, was doing a lot of damage to the Dutch up front but unfortunately, the support wasn't what it might have been. Somehow, this problem had to be addressed in the second half.

The Dutch, as they had done in the first half, attacked us right from the restart and we almost got ourselves in serious trouble when first Ray Houghton and later Steve Staunton lost the ball in midfield. It is in those situations that we are most vulnerable and Holland, as I expected, were not slow to capitalise. On each occasion, they ran us half the length of the pitch and it was all credit to our defence that we managed to escape unpunished.

Other than that, however, we're doing well. Morris and Staunton are at last getting in behind them down the flanks, some good-looking crosses are beginning to go in and when Steve gets one right on target, it seems as if we must score. But

Aldridge is just a split second too late to make contact in front of goal and when the ball runs through to Niall, he's unbalanced. Even the Dutch, I suspect, cannot believe what they're seeing.

Yet, I'm not discouraged. We now have a real presence in the game. Holland are beginning to panic and I notice Wouters on the half-way line bending over trying to get his breath back. The pace of the game is getting to them—we're now paying them back for what they did to us in Germany two years ago.

We still don't have anything to show for it, of course, and with 25 minutes to go, I mention to Maurice that I'm going to make a change and gamble with Ronnie Whelan. To be honest, I'm not absolutely certain of his fitness. But he's a good player on the ball and with Paul McGrath looking after him, he'll not get run too much in midfield. I'll take Kevin Sheedy off and ask Andy Townsend to push on down the left in the hope that at least one of the knock-ons falls kindly for us.

A second change will bring Tony Cascarino into the game in place of John Aldridge and having struggled all night with Quinn, the last thing the Dutch defence wants is to have to contend with a second big man up front. Niall has been a revelation and when the equaliser eventually arrives, it is fitting that he should be the one on the end of it.

Bonner's long accurate kick-out put them under pressure in the first instance and Benny Van Aerle had no real option but to attempt to play the ball back to Van Breukelen. Unfortunately for him, he toe-poked it and instead of going out for a corner, it kicked back rather like a leg-break in cricket, hit the 'keeper in the chest and Quinn was in like a flash to put the rebound in the net. Bloody marvellous!

Some might call it a lucky score but for me it was a goal born of pressure. And there was an element of irony there, too, for the manner in which the ball 'kicked' wasn't wholly dissimilar from the way Wim Kieft scored the winner in Gelsenkirchen.

In or about this time, we hear on the bush telegraph that England are leading 1–0 in Cagliari and if the scorelines in both games stay unaltered, it means that both the Dutch and ourselves will join England in the second phase of the championship. Deliberately, however, I don't tell the players the good news from Cagliari.

For the next five minutes or so, we put Holland under a fair amount of pressure and I recall turning to Maurice Setters and saying 'We're going to win this bloody thing now.' Then Ray Houghton got injured in midfield and while he was having treatment, the word obviously spread among the players that England were beating the Egyptians.

As I said, I consciously refused to give our team the news, but if those of us sitting in the dug-out knew it, it was a racing certainty that the guys out on the pitch would soon get to know it. Then Ruud Gullit walked up to Mick McCarthy, had a few words with him, and from that point nobody attacked anybody.

It certainly wasn't my decision and I doubt if Beenhakker was consulted either. But the players had agreed among themselves that they would settle for the 1–1 draw in the belief that England would hold on to

their lead in Cagliari. At that point, I felt we were going to win the game. But at the end of the day, the only thing that mattered was that we qualify.

The next ten minutes or whatever remained in the game, were the longest I've known in football. In these situations, I don't trust anybody and I kept thinking to myself what happens if we do something silly and the Dutch score. The referee didn't help either by insisting on playing two or three minutes extra time in a situation in which it was apparent to everyone that the teams were now merely going through the motions.

The referee's attitude annoyed me. Had it been a game involving two South American teams, there would have been no hassle about the players knocking the ball to each other at the back. But because European sides were involved and because the tempo of the game had been so hectic for most of the night, he couldn't accept the idea of players taking a 'breather'. That was a classic illustration of the double standards in football.

Eventually, he did blow time and the sense of relief in both camps was obvious. It had been a hard, demanding game for everybody and if there were tough-luck stories on either side, I reckoned that the scoreline was a fair one. Honour had not only been served but was seen to be served. Now we can both look forward to playing in the knock-out stages of the championship.

With England winning against Egypt, it meant that they top the group with four points, leaving the Dutch and ourselves tied for second place with identical points

After the disappointments of the Egypt match, it was good to get back to playing football again against Holland. Here Niall Quinn and Andy Townsend get stuck in.

Big Niall Quinn was the hero of the hour against the Dutch.

The Irish bench before and after Niall Quinn's equaliser against the Dutch. Spot the difference!

Captain courageous. Mick McCarthy shows his delight after the Dutch match. No player has been more unfairly criticised and no player ever gave more to his team than Mick. Now he is entitled to smile. He has just captained Ireland to a draw with Holland which ensures that we have qualified for the second round of the finals.

and goals columns. The FIFA people now had to draw lots to determine second and third places and I was aware that it would take place in Rome within fifteen minutes of our game ending. The outcome of that lottery would be crucial, but I couldn't hang around waiting for it to happen. I had press and television interviews to do.

I had just finished with the television people and as I walked across to the press centre somebody told me that we've been drawn in second place ahead of the Dutch, and will now meet Romania in Genoa for a place in the quarter-finals. For me, this is the icing on the cake— the perfect ending to a night which had done football proud.

It means that Holland will have to face West Germany in the next round, a task I would sooner leave to them. The Romanians, to me, are at this stage a bit of an unknown quantity. But somehow, I'd rather take my chance with them than go in against Franz Beckenbauer's team.

One of the local police people has mentioned that the West German–Holland game will pose a security problem, but I think that's the least of Beenhakker's troubles. On my way back from the press conference, I came almost face to face with Leo and he looked worried. I don't know if he saw me, but if he did he turned and looked away.

I don't know the reason for that but it can't have been anything that happened in the game. As I've already said it represented much that is good in football and the Dutch, like ourselves, can only be proud to have been part of it.

FRIDAY 22
June 1990

●

According to some people, this should have been the day we were returning to Dublin, but neither I nor the lads in the squad ever read it that way. Sure we had been drawn in the toughest of the six qualifying groups, but it was always our belief that we would survive to play on the Italian mainland. In three games on the islands of Sardinia and Sicily, we have conceded just one goal and while we didn't score too many either, I figure that our performance against Holland proved beyond all doubt that we deserve to participate in the knock-out stages of the championship.

Holland may not always have played like reigning European champions, but for many people here they are still potentially one of the most exciting teams of all. The fact that we did so well against them yesterday merely reinforced my belief that when we got our act together we could look anybody in the eye.

Another encouraging feature of the Dutch game was that we avoided serious injury. This is always a major headache for any manager and between Ronnie Whelan and Ray Houghton, we have experienced our fair quota of problems in the build-up to this championship. But in our games to date we have, thankfully, come through relatively unscathed: a major bonus.

The other point which gives me genuine pleasure is that for all our commitment on the pitch, we have picked up just one yellow card—and that for a relatively innocuous tackle by Chris Morris in the England game. The discipline shown by the players has been exemplary and as long as we get a fair crack of the whip from referees, I'll have no worries on this score.

The fact that we are going to Genoa for the Romanian game is another plus. Scotland have been based there for the first phase of the championship and the reports from their camp suggest that when we move into the hotel which they have just vacated in Rapallo, a resort just outside the city, we'll have no complaints.

Because of the early start of the journey to Genoa, there were no late night celebrations last night. Some of the wives stayed overnight in the hotel and, indirectly, they were caught up in the dispute which threatened to delay our departure.

To accommodate the women, it was necessary to alter the rooming arrangements. But since we had booked and paid for double rooms, it ought not have created any problems for the hotel management. But to our amazement, they insisted on charging extra. This we refused to pay.

Overall, our relationship with the hotel people was not the most cordial and they annoyed us further by presenting us with ludicrously high bills for sundries, just as we were about to leave. People who had made collect calls home were now being asked to pay anything up to £80 and the President of the FAI, Fran Fields, was billed for a cool two million lira or £1,000 in our currency.

Things were getting a little out of hand when I discovered that with the players already on the coach, waiting to take them to the airport, the hotel management were refusing to release our luggage, until the bills were paid in full. I asked for volunteers, got ten or twelve lads to work at moving our gear on to the coach and told the Italians that if they still felt a sense of grievance, they could sort it out with FIFA.

Our hotel in Genoa, by contrast, is excellent. Food and drinks awaited us on our arrival here, the rooms are spacious and the Scots were right when they told us that we wouldn't find a more comfortable base in Italy. Mick McCarthy, as team skipper, is delegated by the players to refer any complaints to me and today he has only one moan. He says the place is too nice!

Nice hotel or not, the work goes on and within four hours of our arrival, we're on our way to training. It's optional for those who played last night but the mood of expectancy is now such that everybody wants to participate. We're going to enjoy our stay here.

SATURDAY 23
June 1990

●

We decide to take a look at the match stadium and we're more than a little concerned at what we see. Scotland had played Brazil there in their first phase game and looking in on television, I thought the place was enormous. The reality is somewhat different.

The first thing that strikes us is the proximity of the stands to the pitch. They are tall and sheer and there are no corners or wind channels to provide a draught. It is, for all the world, like a confined rectangular box—certainly not the place I would choose for a game kicking off at five o'clock in this kind of heat.

It is warm this morning, very warm, and if this kind of weather lasts, there is going to be a vast outpouring of sweat on Monday. We check with the met. people and they confirm our worst suspicions. It could be even hotter on match day.

In the afternoon, just to break the monotony of the players hanging about the hotel, I give them permission to go for a ramble down town. I'll be going, too, and I warn them that anybody caught out-doors without a hat, will be fined a tenner. It isn't just an idle threat—I cannot afford the risk of people going down with sunstroke at this stage of the championship.

When I eventually catch up with them, I notice that people like Paul McGrath and John Sheridan are, in fact, hatless, but they're sitting in the shade. I watch to see what happens and as soon as they move out into the direct sunlight, they promptly put their hats back on. That doesn't come easily to young people but it pleases me. It shows that the lads are as alert as I am to the dangers of the sun and they can appreciate fully why the swimming pool at the hotel will remain off-limits.

That afternoon, the tapes of the Romanians' earlier games, which I had requested as soon as I knew that we were going to play them, arrive from Rome. Because of the glut of football on television this last fortnight, games tend to become blurred and as such, the tapes are

invaluable. We watch the Romanians carefully and I jot down a few notes which I feel will be relevant in forming our match strategy.

Like all Eastern European teams, they are technically correct and they knock the ball around accurately. Their build-up is generally unhurried, but once in the top third of the pitch they put their foot on the throttle. More than ever before, we've got to make certain that our cover at the back is adequate.

Against Ireland, Romania must replace Marius Lacatus, their aggressive midfield player who is suspended for one game after picking up two yellow cards. I liked what I saw of Lacatus on the videos. He was strong and competitive going down the flanks and the lad obviously possesses a flair for scoring. I don't know what his replacement will be like but the change must improve our prospects of winning a place in the quarter-finals.

The goalkeeper, Lunig, looks a very competent lad and I am also taken by the performances of Popescu at centre back. Not only did he do his basic duties to perfection, but when the opportunity presented itself, he was prepared to run the length of the pitch. Big men coming through at his pace can strike terror into even the bravest defender.

Yet the Romanian player who impressed me most—and I suspect the reaction, world-wide, was much the same—is Gheorghe Hagi. For me, he is far and away the best player I have seen in the competition to date, a gifted ball player who can strike the ball with tremendous power with his left foot.

I look at my notes at the end of the evening and see that I have mentioned Hagi and that famous left peg of his on no fewer than four occasions. Somehow we must close him down on that side and make him operate on his weaker leg. If we don't, he can sink us.

SUNDAY 24
June 1990

●

I tell the press people that I am still chewing over my team selection. But in fact, I've already made up my mind that I'll go with an unchanged side from that which played Holland. A couple of players are still carrying minor injuries and the two full backs, Chris Morris and Steve Staunton, are, as ever, high on the list of players requiring treatment from Mick Byrne.

Morris has been carrying a suspect ankle since day one, but providing he does not overdo things in training, he seems to get through games without too much difficulty. I'm keeping my fingers crossed that nothing goes wrong for him now, for he has had a good championship to date and we need all our resources at the back to cope with Hagi and his mates.

Ronnie Whelan did reasonably well when he came off the bench for the last quarter of the Dutch game and will again be included among the five substitutes. But at this stage, there is no question of altering the midfield formation which has been quite magnificent since arriving in Italy.

We go to the stadium for training, still full of apprehension about the weather and it

is again uncomfortably warm. Because of the lack of wind circulating around the place, even the slightest movement is taxing but we comfort ourselves in the knowledge that the Romanians are also certain to find the going tough in there.

Back at the hotel, it is again necessary to ban sunbathing at the pool. The card players have no problem in settling themselves indoors but I feel genuinely sorry for those who wish to work on their swimming.

In the afternoon, we watch Argentina beat Brazil on television and share the general sense of shock. The Brazilians are still the most exciting spectacle in football and with their exit from the competition some believe that the World Cup has already lost its soul.

Over the 90 minutes, they give the Argentinians a lesson in some of the game's finer points, hit the woodwork on three occasions but still end up on the wrong end of the scoreline. There is a sharp lesson there for those who believe that football is all about doing the pretty thing and entertaining with deft ball control.

There is, of course, a high place for skill and attractive approach play. But when you get right down to it, it is goals which count. And the lessons of the game in Turin today are that the Brazilians, for all their exciting movement, lacked the ability to convert possession into the hard currency of goals.

I felt that we could draw some useful conclusions from the Brazilians' fate. Their style of football is not ours for there are few countries in the world who can hope to match them when it comes to athleticism and the flair for doing the unexpected.

Like Brazil, however, I believe that we have been less than economical with our scoring opportunities and that must change. At this level of competition, you get only so many chances in and around the six yards area and you must make them count. Failure to do so will always give the opposition the opportunity of clawing their way back into the game and Claudio Caniggia's late winner for Argentina made the point perfectly in Turin.

Tonight, Maurice Setters and I were joined by some journalist friends over a few drinks and we relived the bitter experiences of the Brazilians. The World Cup might be the poorer for their going but it opens up all kinds of possibilities for those of us remaining in the championship. If we need any extra incentive going into the game against Romania tomorrow, this is it.

MONDAY 25
June 1990

●

The usual match day arrangements apply with a light lunch and then a short rest before Mick Byrne assembles the squad and gets them on to the coach taking them to the stadium. On our way there, we are again stunned by the huge number of Irish fans on their way to the match.

We were told that many of those who accompanied us to Sardinia and Sicily had returned home but if that was the case— and we noticed many familiar faces in the

crowd—ample reinforcements had arrived from Ireland. There seemed to be green flags and green shirts everywhere and that was a source of consolation for what we knew would be a difficult day's work.

The Romanian colours were, predictably, less conspicuous but at the end of the day, that wouldn't make our task any easier. The work would still have to be done out on the grass and no amount of vocal support would change that. As normal, the players put on their warm-up gear before boarding the coach, so that they were ready to go on to the pitch once they arrived in the stadium.

In fact, I didn't allow them do so. I knew the place was going to be hot, but even I hadn't legislated fully for the conditions which awaited us. It was boiling out there and there was nothing to be gained by allowing the lads to expend unnecessary energy. Mercifully the dressing rooms were air conditioned and in those circumstances it seemed wiser to undertake our preparations indoors.

As usual, there were a few dissenters and again there was no way I could stop either of the goalkeepers going out and doing their pre-match routine. Three or four of the players who wouldn't be involved in the game went out to help them while the remainder of us prepared ourselves mentally for the match.

When it eventually started, I wasn't particularly impressed with our early performance. We were too sluggish for my peace of mind, and if I hadn't known better I would have said that they had eaten too much at lunch. It is funny the things which run through your mind at times like that, but watching our players struggle, it seemed to me that we were totally uncoordinated.

We are normally strongest in the opening twenty minutes of the game, but here we were getting the run-around by the Romanians at a time when I anticipated that we would be turning the screws on them. We weren't getting in fast enough to close them down and while we were still attempting to adjust to the pace of things, we might have gone a couple of goals down.

On at least two occasions, they ran us the length of the pitch and most ominously of all, we weren't coping with Hagi nearly as well as I had hoped. As a matter of policy, we had decided against man-marking him—the player closest to him at any particular time would pick him up—but in the event, we were doing neither.

All those warnings about the need to close him down on his left foot appeared to have been forgotten and on at least three occasions, he found the time and the room to swing that trusty boot. Fortunately for us, he was 25 or 30 yards from goal at the time but the power of the man was such that Paddy Bonner still had to look smart to keep the shots out.

Then, almost as suddenly, the pattern of the match changed. Our lads discovered what the Romanians were about, sorted out the problems and after that, I never considered that we would lose. Unfortunately, John Aldridge was in the 'wars' early on and after damaging an achilles tendon, he had to be replaced by Tony Cascarino.

It was always my intention that Cascarino would get a run at some stage. But I hadn't figured on an emergency like this. It meant that we had to use one of our two substitutes much earlier than I had planned and that reduced our options dramatically.

Yet I was encouraged by the way we had fought our way back into contention. Paul McGrath and Andy Townsend were beginning to make their presence felt in central midfield and for the first time in the game, Ray Houghton and Kevin Sheedy were beginning to get at them down the flanks.

Once again, however, the breaks weren't going our way and every time Niall Quinn or Cascarino won the ball in the air, it seemed to fall to a Romanian. The exception materialised just before half-time and it was as close as we were to come to scoring all day.

When Cascarino eventually nodded one on for Sheedy, it seemed as if we must score. But Kevin, at full stretch, saw his flick strike the goalkeeper on the arm and run past the post. Hagi, drifting more and more towards the wings, still looked dangerous in the second half but overall ours were the better scoring opportunities in that period.

Big Niall was just off target with a header and there were a couple of times when the ball ran across the face of the Romanian goalmouth in situations in which it needed only a touch to put it in. Oddly enough, I always felt that we would score. But as it transpired, it was not to be and the game went into extra time.

In conditions like these, the last thing we wanted was to have to play an additional

△ A view of the Irish bench during the Romanian game. As you can see, we all look pretty thoughtful.

△ Steve Staunton in hot pursuit.

Kevin Sheedy takes on two Romanians.

△   Andy Townsend ran and ran – all through the finals. The Romania game was no exception.

△   Before the penalty shoot-out against Romania, I went round and had a word with each of the lads. In this photograph, I'm on the left-hand side.

30 minutes, but now that we were confronted with the challenge, I felt that we were better prepared to cope with it than the opposition. We had planned on slowing the game down at times to give ourselves a 'breather' but in the event we didn't have to do so. The Romanians did it for us. They, too, were feeling the effects of the sun and on occasions deliberately played the ball across the back four to take the pace out of the match. We didn't object. People in the stands may not have found it wildly exciting but then, they didn't have to go chasing about under a sun like this.

There was an incident just before the end of ordinary time when I got a dressing-down by the Brazilian referee, Ramos Wright, and subsequently a strongly worded warning from FIFA about my future conduct after I had walked towards the touchline to remonstrate with the referee for booking Paul McGrath.

McGrath, a scrupulously fair competitor, had tackled Hagi perfectly legally and I saw red when Wright reached into his pocket and produced the yellow card to him. It was perhaps the only time in the game that Paul was stretching in the tackle and I simply couldn't believe it when he was booked.

Aldridge had been similarly disciplined in the first half, but in his case we could have no complaints: he was unquestionably late in the tackle. The McGrath incident was wholly different, however, and I felt justified in making my feelings known to the referee.

In fact, it was the culmination of a running battle with the match officials. Before the match, they insisted that I sit on the bench but I refused to do so for the very good reason that I couldn't see the bloody game from there. Moreover, there was a television cameraman standing immediately to my right who obscured my view of the play down that side of the field.

Every time I turned around, he had his camera poked in my face and at one point I asked him if he had come to watch the game or me. Television runs the show these days, but I object strenuously to the situation in which cameramen are free to go anywhere they like on the pitch while managers are confined to the bench. I won that particular battle but I'm afraid I lost out on the McGrath affair.

Deciding that discretion was the better part of valour and that I had already pushed Wright as far as he was prepared to go, I dutifully took my place on the bench and sat there suffering, just like everybody else, as the game went into extra time.

We pushed for a winner in that period and I thought we always looked more likely to get it than Romania. But try as we would, we just couldn't open up their defence and as the minutes ticked away, I thought, bloody hell, we're into a sudden death penalty shoot-out.

Shoot-outs are great when you win them, savage in the extreme when luck runs against you. But my first thoughts when the referee spread his arms wide and indicated that we would now go to penalties, were entirely positive. The fact that we could lose it simply never occurred to me. Wright indicated that I could now walk on to the pitch to talk to the players if I wished and, of course, I needed no second invitation.

The lads were sitting there pretty well exhausted and I just went to them and said that whatever happened in the next few minutes, they had done the country proud. I had no idea who would take the kicks, apart from the fact that Kevin Sheedy would hit the first one. But I was conscious of the fact that two of the players most skilled in that department, John Aldridge and Ronnie Whelan, were sitting on the bench.

I asked Kevin what he intended to do and he told me he'd blast it over the 'keeper's head. I said, 'Go ahead and sock it to them' and he just smiled wanly. Then the referee summoned the first Romanian to the penalty spot and all Ireland held its breath.

By this stage I was back on the bench. Some of the kicks I watched on the giant television screen overlooking the stadium, purely because I could see things better that way. But, strangely enough, I wasn't nervous.

I did get angry, however, when I saw the referee stop Sheedy and Ray Houghton after they had placed the ball, to check their numbers. I thought he was completely out of order, for at that point he was liable to break their concentration. If numbers had to be checked, the time to do it was when they walked up to place it. Fortunately, the lads kept their minds on the job and we matched Romania penalty for penalty with the first four kicks.

Then the real drama. The Romanians entrusted their last kick to Daniel Timofte, a lad who had come into the game as a second-half replacement, and as it turned out, it proved a critical decision. He struck the ball well enough but Bonner, a mite unlucky not to have stopped one of the earlier shots, read the line perfectly and diving to his right, parried it at the post. Superb.

Pakie thumped the ground in delight, hauled himself off the grass, and like every Irish supporter in the ground, my eyes moved almost instinctively back to the centre circle to see who was going to take the last vital kick for us. I'm as much in the dark as anybody and I must confess that I'm a little taken aback when I see big David O'Leary striding up towards the penalty area.

As one of the old school, I've never considered centre backs to be among the best kickers of a penalty and as far as I know, David hasn't taken one for years. But the big fellow strides on, puts the ball down and hoofs it into the roof of the net.

It wasn't the best penalty I've ever seen but for my money it was the most vital and as soon as the ball is safely in the netting, O'Leary is mobbed by his teammates. What a moment for him. I certainly wouldn't have swapped places with him as he ran up to that kick, but his nerve held and the rest is history.

I look at the Romanians and my heart goes out to them. To lose any World Cup game is galling but to go out in these circumstances is absolutely heart breaking. What can I say that will lessen the pain? Then I look at the sheer joy on the faces of the Irish people around me, and I realise that what we've just seen will adorn Irish sporting history for ever.

TUESDAY 26
June 1990

●

The show is on the road early for we are told that we must be at the airport at something like ten o'clock to catch a flight to Rome for Saturday's quarter-final appointment with Italy. Unlike Palermo, we leave our headquarters in Genoa with regret for our stay there has been truly delightful, with the hotel management doing everything possible to facilitate us.

Unfortunately, the respite from hotel problems is only temporary for when we get to Rome, we discover the quarters reserved for us by FIFA are far from satisfactory. We are to be based in Nemi, a village set in the Colli Albani hills some thirty miles outside the city, where the American squad was housed before us. Ironically, the Italian team is encamped just a couple of kilometres down the road in Marino but I bet their hotel is more accommodating that this.

The place is small and what they've gone and done is to convert single rooms into doubles. There just isn't room to turn and when the players see them, they say no way. So, we go to inspect another hotel in the area and discover that it is even less satisfactory. We return to the first place and set about the task of making the best of a bad lot.

By shifting people around, we are able to give the players single rooms with the bigger lads getting double beds. This appealed to people like Niall Quinn, Paddy Bonner and Gerry Peyton for they are not a pretty sight, spilling half-way out of bed.

We go to train at a local ground and are confronted by a small army of journalists. The Italians have discovered us. 'The Little Invincibles', as one paper described us, have arrived in town and suddenly, we are in greater demand by the media than at any time since leaving home.

Before this, we were probably nothing more than a curiosity to the Italian press but to judge by the number of television and print journalists now turning up, they are obviously intent on putting that to rights. The next three or four days threaten to be hectic.

We, for our part, have some catching up to do in our homework on the Italian team. We've watched them on television: we are aware of the guys to look out for but now, for the first time, we are required to condense that information into a viable match plan. So, tonight we make a start on operation Schillaci.

WEDNESDAY 27
June 1990

●

Mick Byrne is one of the great characters in the Ireland entourage. A skilled physiotherapist, he was involved with the team long before I arrived on the scene and enjoys a special relationship with the players, particularly the older ones. He is also a deeply religious man and when I was appointed, I promised him that I would get him to Rome in four years' time to see the Pope.

That undertaking was given with more hope than confidence, it has to be said, but now, here we are in the Eternal City and we're right on cue to deliver on the pledge. Monsignor Liam O'Boyle, who has been saying Mass for the party since we arrived here, is a man with some influence in the Vatican and he promised to do what he could to make Mick's dream a reality.

The Monsignor is also a man of his word and no sooner had we set down in Rome than he confirmed that the papal audience was on and that we were to present ourselves in the Vatican on Wednesday morning. We would be there as part of a general audience but in the hope that we might get to have a few words with His Holiness, we were advised to wear our official uniforms.

In fact, we did just that. When we walked in, we got an ovation from the rest of the people there and were taken to some seats in the front. Eventually, we were presented to the Pontiff and after Mick Byrne had given him a football autographed by the players, he shook hands with each of us.

When I was introduced, he just said, 'Ah, Mr Charlton, the boss' and smiled. As a former goalkeeper himself, he seemed to take a particular interest in Paddy Bonner and Gerry Peyton but the person who undoubtedly took his fancy was little Charlie O'Leary. He talked at length to Charlie but the sense of awe was such that Charlie cannot remember a word he said.

As a non-Catholic, I found it a very moving experience and the privilege was, of course, magnified for the Catholics among us. Alan McLoughlin and Bernie Slaven must have been particularly impressed, for they got lost in the place and eventually kept us waiting 15 minutes while various search parties were dispatched to find them.

This evening, some of our players take part in a drugs awareness programme which is being televised, both nationally and internationally. Paddy Bonner and Chris Hughton do the honours and, as I expected, they acquit themselves well.

THURSDAY 28
June 1990

●

A routine day at the office. Our main preoccupation is with the fitness of John Aldridge, Steve Staunton and Tony Cascarino. John is the most doubtful of the trio, for the tendon injury sustained in the Romanian game is still very sore and clearly he is going to struggle to make it in time.

In normal circumstances, we would be talking of a recovery period of at least a week but this is probably the most important football game Ireland has ever played and everybody wants to be part of it. That desire has got to be tempered with caution, however, for we cannot afford to go with players who are less than 100% fit.

Staunton, who had to be replaced in the game against Romania, and Cascarino, are both showing signs of recovery but no less that Aldo, they're going to have to convince me that they are capable of lasting the full 90 minutes on Saturday.

By now, we have run through the videos of Italy's earlier games and they confirm what we already know. They are a very accomplished side with scarcely a weak link anywhere and the fact that they have not conceded a goal in 360 minutes of World Cup football speaks volumes about the character and commitment of their players.

The name on everybody's lips is Salvatore Schillaci—and no wonder! He has kept the great Gianluca Vialli out of the team since the start of the competition and the way he is playing, we may need to build a brick wall to contain him. But Mick McCarthy and Kevin Moran have handled big name players in the past—they won't be losing any sleep at the prospect of marking Schillaci.

McCarthy, in particular, is having a marvellous tournament and I wonder again about the knowledge of the critics who, before we came out here, were predicting all kinds of gloom and doom in the centre of our defence. Perhaps I've missed something that these people see but as I view it we have the bravest and most reliable centre backs in the business.

That said, I'm not underestimating the threat of Schillaci. The guy has the eyes of a fugitive and he's just as cunning when it comes to drifting away from his marker. Yes, he'll require a lot of watching now but the player who really takes my fancy is the boy, Donadoni.

I watched him in the game against Czechoslovakia and again in the match with Uruguay and I thought he was brilliant. He's the lad who puts it all together for them in the middle of the park. He's the one who could bring it all toppling down on our heads now.

FRIDAY 29
June 1990

●

Went down to the Olympic Stadium in Rome—what a place! I've been here before, of course, but since they've reconstructed it the sense of spaciousness is now more imposing than ever. This is the stadium where the World Cup final will be played and as we arrive, the thought crosses my mind—will we be coming back here in a week's time?

I'm aware that the possibility hasn't even dawned on the hundreds of journalists now gathered at the entrance to the stadium but that doesn't bother me unduly. I know a lot more about my team than they do and I've seen enough to convince me that we're not a million miles from achieving what they consider to be the unachievable.

When it comes down to character, we've got as much as anybody. But will we be allowed to beat the Italians? Eliminating the host country has never been easy in any World Cup championship and judged on the fanaticism I've seen in this country, it's going to take a brave set of match officials to rule against them in 50–50 situations. We can live with that but the crunch will come if we go a goal up on them.

Maurice Setters and I have already been through that scenario but we keep our thoughts to ourselves as the press people gather around us. We train for 45 minutes— then the injured lads take part in stretching and running exercises. They come through fairly well but I stress that I will not be making up my mind on their fitness until the morning of the game.

There must be a hundred or more journalists at the press conference and they ask me the same elementary questions over and over again. We've been in Italy now for three weeks but as far as they're concerned, we might only have just arrived. I find it all a bit irritating but I bite my lip and attempt to be as plausible as I can with the answers.

In the hotel this afternoon, we watch more videos of the Italians. The players, strangely, are not too keen on watching televised football, presumably because they get enough of the real thing. But on this occasion, they are rapt in their attention. There is a certain amount of tension in the room because now, for the first time, perhaps, they realise they are very much the underdogs going into the game. We discuss the Italian team, individually and collectively, at half-time and again at the end of the video and the mood is sombre.

Later in the day, a consignment of Guinness arrives from the Irish embassy in Rome and seeing that the evening is balmy, we decide to have a few drinks out on the forecourt of the hotel. The tension is getting to the backroom boys as much as the players and this seems as good a way as any of letting off steam.

There is nothing rowdy and very little raucous about our little party but at 11 o'clock or thereabouts, I get a message down from Mick McCarthy that we're making too much noise and that the players cannot get to sleep. I had forgotten

that they were roomed towards the front of the building and McCarthy was, of course, justified in making the complaint.

We moved inside and Mick later told us that it was as if somebody had switched off the television. We drank on for another half an hour or so and then retired for the night. Tomorrow will be a long, eventful day for everybody.

SATURDAY 30
June 1990

●

Maurice had arranged to take Aldridge, Cascarino and Staunton out early to put them through their fitness tests and before the rest of us were quite awake, they were gone. I was so worried about their condition that I tried to talk them out of playing. I told them that if they had to come off after 20 or 25 minutes, they would undo the whole team plan. If they made themselves available for selection, they must be convinced in their own minds that they could last out the full game. All three of them informed me with as much conviction as they could muster that they would be fine and I had to be influenced by that.

Back at the hotel, Setters and I sat under a tree out in the grounds and went through the pros and cons of the various alternatives. I was seriously tempted to play Chris Hughton at left back, not just because of the doubts about Staunton's damaged hamstring but because the man's form in the build-up programme was impressive.

Chris would do a good job for us in any game; against that, however, I was aware of the need to preserve the balance and the basic structure of the team. Steve, as I said previously, has one of the best left pegs in the business. This was a match in which we would need all his accuracy in playing the ball into the corners, so I decided to stick with him.

I also had genuine doubts whether I would play John Aldridge. I was concerned about his injury but, more than that, we might need the extra bit of pace which David Kelly, for example, could give us across the front. The counter-argument was that David hadn't yet played in the championship and this might be a risky game in which to throw him in. I eventually decided to go with John.

With those two issues settled, I had no problems in completing the teamsheet. It was the same as that for the last two games with John Sheridan joining Ronnie Whelan on the bench, because we might need a change of direction in midfield at some stage.

After finishing with the selection, we got to talking about the game itself. I think we both had a deep sense of foreboding. Football is football and nobody can legislate for the freak bounce of the ball or the misplaced pass which can undo even the most carefully laid plans. But sitting there in the quiet of the garden, we knew that we could expect no favours from anybody tonight.

Italy are the glamour team of the championship and if they go out, it loses at least some of its appeal. From a purely mercenary point of view, it will be bad

business if Azeglio Vicini, the Italian manager, fails to deliver the win.

A Portuguese referee had been appointed to take charge of the match and that was another source of worry. I don't like referees from that part of the world because they don't see the game in the same way we do in Britain or Ireland. Things we consider are OK, they generally don't like. Ours is a physical game based on competition and pressure, but it's just the kind of game which makes most Latin referees suspicious.

When we eventually got to the precincts of the ground, there was a bit of a hiccup with the tapes being played on the coach and I had a go at Charlie O'Leary. Instead of Sean South from Garryowen, this dreadful dirge about lowering somebody or other into the ground came on. And I hated it. I remembered it well from a visit to Poland four years ago when Charlie again played it by mistake and we lost the game 1–0. It's an error I could have done without now.

The Olympic Stadium is unusual in the sense that when you drive in, you turn up an alley way, then through a tunnel beneath the stand and when you eventually emerge into daylight, there, just a couple of yards ahead of you, is the pitch. It hits you just as quickly and as suddenly as that. We walked the few yards to the dressing room, did our team talk and then went out to warm up. The closing stages of the Argentina–Yugoslavia game were being shown on the television screen in the stadium and after limbering up, the lads just squatted in the centre circle and watched the action on the big screen. I could not believe that everybody was so relaxed.

Then the Italians came out, we exchanged greetings and they also wanted to take a look at the opponents one or other of us would be meeting in the semi-final at Naples next Tuesday. After all the hype, all the pressures of the last few days, we might as well have been getting ready for a scratch game on the village green.

Gradually and, perhaps inevitably, the mood changed when we got back to the dressing room and as we sat there waiting for the referee to come knocking on the door, there was a lot of tension. The game plan was unequivocal. We would take the game to them, have a go at their defence and, above all, cut down our margin of error at the back.

The first part, I thought, we did perfectly for 20 minutes or so. We pulled the ball down in midfield, moved it with speed and accuracy and in that period, people like Kevin Sheedy, Paul McGrath and Ray Houghton probably played better than at any time in the championship. The Italian defence, as I expected, was disciplined but I'd seen nothing in the game so far to suggest that it was unwinnable in the normal sense.

Then, in moments of sheer madness, everything is undone. Kevin Sheedy wins a ball on the left and as John Aldridge comes to 'show' for the pass, everybody is moving forward. Sadly, for us, Fernando De Napoli makes the interception before it reaches Aldo and the rest is tragedy.

For once, we are caught bare across midfield and the Italians, brilliant on the counter, exact full retribution. They run us

threequarters the length of the pitch, going left, but there is still a chance that we can escape until the ball reaches Donadoni. He checks, comes inside and then produces a 'rocket' from just inside the penalty area.

Bonner loses his footing momentarily, parries the shot and then, fatefully, slips again as the rebound runs to Schillaci and with all the conviction of a man who can do no wrong at this particular time, he puts it in the net. All hell breaks loose and I curse, undeniably curse.

From an Italian point of view, it was a fine score for they finished it brilliantly. But it was a bad goal to concede. Time and again, I had warned our fellows that the only games they would lose would be those in which we passed the ball unnecessarily across midfield or, alternatively, played balls in risky situations to the feet.

The Italian score fell into the second category. Instead of looking for the ball to be played to his feet, Aldridge, I felt, ought to have been running. And once the initial mistake had been made, we were in serious trouble. What made it all the more galling was the fact that it was the only occasion on which they seriously threatened us in the first half.

Bergomi missed with a header and Schillaci turned one over the top in a situation in which the ball was running away from him but apart from that one crucial mistake, I reckoned that we had given as good as we got in the opening 45 minutes. At that point, all was far from lost.

There was one later occasion when we were fortunate after Schillaci struck the underside of the crossbar with a smashing shot but it was the only time that they

Two views of Mick McCarthy in action against Italy.

Steve Staunton challenges Donadoni.

Schillaci celebrates!

Tony Cascarino in the thick of things. Franco Baresi makes his feelings known!

After the Italy match everyone saluted the fans, including Niall Quinn and Steve Staunton (above) and Charlie Haughey (below).

looked likely to extend their lead. For much of the time, we were putting the bite on them, playing neat, controlled football across midfield and generally giving the lie yet again to those who maintained that we were incapable of putting four or five passes together.

We were winning the battle for midfield control now but every time it seemed that we competed for the ball in any kind of doubtful situation, the referee whistled for a foul against us. I mean there were many times when there seemed to be clear daylight between one of our players and an Italian and yet he still gave them a free kick.

That kind of thing is soul destroying for any team. You think you have won the ball cleanly and fairly and the referee goes and takes it from you to give it back to the opposition. In these circumstances, it's very difficult for us to develop any real momentum. And that simply infuriated me. I genuinely believed that we had the players and the resources to win the game. I could still 'smell' the final but suddenly we were beginning to run out of time.

Eventually, the referee gave us a free kick close to their 18 yards line after Tony Cascarino had been blatantly pushed but at this stage, it's all but too late. Paul McGrath has one shot which flies across the goalmouth and wide but I'm afraid that time and the referee had run out on us. The adventure is over—we're on our way back to Dublin!

Right now, I'm more angry than sad. A cameraman gets in my way and I give him short shrift. What a time to go sticking a camera in my face. I tell the players I'm proud of them and the

manner in which they have conducted themselves on and off the park. And when I go to the post-match press conference, I say the diplomatic things about the Italians and wish them luck on the rest of their journey.

I deliberately refuse to criticise the referee publicly. In my heart of hearts, I had expected no better and when reporters press me on the subject, I still hold my peace. Then, this guy stands up and asks me to comment on a statement by Azeglio Vicini that his team will have to be protected by referees for the remainder of the championship.

I look him straight in the eye and respond, 'Remember, it was Vicini who said that— not me.'

Because of the dense crowds on the exit roads from the stadium, the journey back to Nemi is long and tortuous and as I look around the coach, I see the faces of men who have left a month's sweat on a field in Rome. Defeat leaves its mark but there is pride, too, and just a trace of bitterness at the way the game was handled.

But soon the despondency lifts and as the bus edges through the hotel gates, we discover that the party which will last long into the night is already under way. Many of the supporters who have brought such credit to the country in the last couple of weeks have preceded us here. For them, as much as the players, it is an occasion for celebration.

Tomorrow, the people of Ireland may pass their judgment on what has been an extraordinary adventure but now, in the sultry heat of a June night in Italy, we're going to have our own shindig.

At times, the hype has been enormous but for all the pressures on 22 players thrown together and living out of each other's pockets for the greater part of seven weeks, there has not been one single falling out. That is a fact which gives me immense pleasure.

Now, as I look out at the celebrations, I feel, perhaps, a greater sense of fulfilment than at any time in my thirty-odd years in the game. We may not have won the World Cup but I like to think that in a very real sense, all of us, players, officials and supporters, restored some of the old, decent values to the game. And in so doing, we may, perhaps, have left our mark on the development of football in the years ahead.

Would I do it again? In four years' time I'll be 58 and the lessons of Italia '90 are that the responsibilities of managing a team in the finals of the World Cup are enormous. I'll go away and think about it and, depending on what happens over the next year or so, make a value judgment.

Make no mistake about it, it's been bloody hard work for everybody but at the end of the day, I felt privileged to serve with a marvellous bunch of players and to have helped, in some small way, boost the image of Ireland and its people. Now, where did I leave that fishing rod?

It's that man again. The Taoiseach welcomes me back from Rome.

△   Down O'Connell Street....

△   .... and into College Green.

Did Kevin leave his front tooth behind in Italy?

Welcome home Paul.